TOWERS

TOWERS

ARCHIE GORDON

With a Foreword by
SIR JOHN BETJEMAN

DAVID & CHARLES
Newton Abbot   London   North Pomfret (Vt)

Frontispiece: the Glenfinnan Monument

ISBN 0 7153 7787 6

© Archie Gordon, Marquess of Aberdeen, 1979

Type set by Trade Linotype Limited, Birmingham
and printed in Great Britain
by Biddles Limited, Guildford
for David & Charles (Publishers) Limited
Brunel House Newton Abbot Devon

Published in the United States of America
by David & Charles Inc
North Pomfret Vermont 05053 USA

CONTENTS

FOREWORD

I am glad Archie Gordon has asked me to write a foreword to this book. Towers give a place identity and are most important in an age which is becoming increasingly anonymous. Tower blocks, those inhuman devices of modern architects, have got towers a bad name. This book, except for the hideous Post Office Tower, will redress the balance. The publishers, I suppose, thought of it as a picture book but as soon as I started reading it I realised it was the personal response of a literate and critical man to the variety of landscape and its adornment in England, Scotland, Wales and Ireland.

Archie Gordon started his career with the Council for the Protection of Rural England. He then became a producer of 'steam radio' as it is called by us who like television. In this capacity Archie had to persuade people to cut out all needless words. Readers will discover he has an eye for architecture and for country and can communicate his enthusiasm and deep knowledge.

When I first met him he was Gilbert Harding's producer. As Gilbert was, he is humorous, opinionated and kind. Humour is a sense of proportion and that is essential to towers. It is also an explanation of the knowledgeable choice of subjects.

I am sorry that he has not included what remains of one of London's most distinguished group of towers. This was T. E. Colcutt's Imperial Institute in South Kensington, built between 1887 and 1893. Only the bell tower, with its 12 bells, remains. The rest has been replaced by London University with dull stuff. The real brick in this Spanish baroque tower contrasts beautifully with the white Portland stone. The brick represents the blood of the soldiers whose subscriptions paid for it. What is still there is symbolic; I suppose what has needlessly gone is also symbolic of our age.

Archie Gordon, to my delighted surprise, inherited a Scottish peerage. He is the Marquess of Aberdeen. This is a very good thing because it means we have in the House of Lords a defender of architecture and landscape, when we are still mourning the deaths of the Earl of Antrim and the Earl of Rosse, who spent so much of their lives in defending both.

Sir John Betjeman

INTRODUCTION

Few of the towers shown and described in these pages owe anything to the natural and manmade features characteristic of the landscapes of the British Isles. These characteristics are in the main an intricate and unobtrusive patchwork of gentle dapplings and inter-woven patterns which merge and change and re-form almost imperceptibly. Some of these patterns have survived, through the geology, from primitive nature; most of them are formed by the restless and changing embroiderings of man. Sharp drops and declivities are certainly present, but not so sharp nor so harsh as those in most other lands. Natural towers are few, and those few are freaks of geology and erosion.

Especially with large buildings, many of the towers I have chosen, by caprice and personal fancy, are only the vertical part of a predominantly horizontal structure evolved in many cases through centuries. They do a certain violence to the scene in which they are set, or even to the buildings from which they ascend, and it is my instinct that this is why they were erected. It makes no difference whether they are surrounded by higher natural features, as the church tower of Widecombe in the Moor, which, high though it be, is dwarfed by the high moors of Dartmoor, or as in the case of Craigievar Castle in Aberdeenshire, command-ing a valley but surrounded by hills; or whether they are set in an almost flat landscape like the mighty Boston Stump near the Lincolnshire coast, or upon a high eminence like the squat, lonely Smailholm Tower in the Borders.

These last two command not only extensive views from their summit, but are also and more importantly, a landmark, or a bearing for seafarers, for miles round. These particular qualities make a strong appeal to me, for I am a great one for a view, and for knowing where I am, and they explain a part of what must seem to some a rather dotty choice.

When I was a small child our home was on the edge of Dartford Heath, an extensive tract of tall gorse and hawthorn and birch, criss-crossed by sandy paths worn through the heather and the rabbit-shaved turf. This is where Greater London laps the shores of Kent, or vice versa. Our nurse was detailed to take us for healthy walks on this heath, and at first it was easy for the little party to lose its way. Then Nannie's Chimney came into view. This was a tall structure somewhere within a large high-fenced area, probably once part of the Heath, and was the most prominent feature of the L.C.C.'s Bexley Mental Hospital. Occasionally it gave out a plume of smoke, and always it gave us our position. 'Look, there's Nannie's Chimney—now we know which way to go'.

The Shot Tower, London

To my myopic childish vision it had the outline of a castle tower. Nannie would wheel round in another direction when she saw it likely that we should pass too close to one of the long, sad lines of patients out walking under escort, the sexes separated, the men in dark, drab clothes and uniformly pale of face; the women more chattery and colourful, with their wispy flutterings of tattered finery, and more heightened complexions. We children were disappointed, wanted a closer look, but her course was set on an avoiding tack, and as often as not it was only when the lunatics' warming chimney came into view that we could judge the way home.

Before I went to school I knew the height of Mount Everest, Aconcagua, many others—Mt. Elbrus in the Caucasus being my trick choice for Europe's highest mountain, to annoy Alp lovers. The attraction of tall towers followed, and started with the Woolworth and the Flat Iron Buildings in New York. The love, and a little knowledge, of our own British towers, came later. Here at last it has the chance of expression, loosely brought together in this selection, which makes no pretence at scholarly appraisal, at guidebook comparisons of excellence, or of being chosen by any other criterion than that of my own peculiar. Perhaps it is I that should be in the crocodile of walkers on Dartford Heath.

By this weird exposition of my reasoning, or lack of it, I am brought fairly to the mention of follies. Scattered about the British Isles, and mostly in England, they are held to be unique as an expression of a rich man's eccentricity. They are mostly 18th century and early 19th; though there are some both earlier and later in date. Some of those chosen are hardly towers, but who could resist a pineapple in Scotland or 'an Obleix to answer a Vistoe' in Ireland?

The choice of castles, particularly from among the Anglo-Norman and Plantagenet strongholds, has been a worry. They all have towers, but often too many, strung out along horizontal curtain walls, for the purpose of isolating a strong vertical emphasis in the landscape. In their time they must have been more frightening than impregnable to the less sophisticated natives whose independent way of life they were designed to suppress—rather as some animals, when confronted by a predator, can puff themselves out, make faces almost, to ward off mortal danger. Today these embattled remains take on for us a more picturesque aspect, more like heavy jewels on the face of the land. There is a phrase of the late Barbara Jones, so perceptive in these matters, when she referred to 'a tiara of castellations'.

I will excuse myself for one obvious omission, and one only : the Tower of London. All through the 900th anniversary year of 1978 I saw hordes of children being marshalled through Tower Hill Underground Station, and I did not envy them their educational treat. Twice I was taken there as a child, and on both occasions got into trouble, even to the point of being warned of what had happened long ago in this fortress, royal palace, prison and place of execution. I liked better the London Zoo; best of all a matinee watching the beautiful ladies and gentlemen of the theatre. The Tower is too well known to need any more remarks from me, except to hope that the citizens of tomorrow have got more benefit from their visit than I did from mine.

No modern tower blocks come into these pages, except as unavoidable backgrounds, because almost none of them seems to me to obey all three of the architectural commandments of Commodity, Firmness and Delight, which cannot be restated too often. In addition planning theory and regulation almost always site them wrongly.

Absent, too, are absent friends. No building not extant at the time of writing is included. Unhappily London's famous Shot Tower on the south bank of the Thames, is no more; neither is Sir Hugh Casson's delightful Skylon of the 1951 London Festival, which was never designed to remain as a permanent structure.

The Skylon, London

Irish Round Towers

The early Christian Round Towers of Ireland must be the oldest mortared buildings in the British Isles, save for the few examples remaining of Roman work. Their survival of up to 1,500 years of Atlantic weather and the behaviour of man owes a lot to the introduction of lime mortar by the Christian missionaries who came from the Roman world in the fifth century. A great deal is also due to their ingenious construction.

Some are complete though not entirely original; some are ruinous. Sixty-five identifiably survive. It has been said that they are only grown up clacháns, the drystone hut dwellings of antiquity, but that is too modest. They were put up beside the low buildings of monasteries to the glory of God and for the better safety of His humble servants in time of danger.

The original towers are remarkably standardised in style and dimensions. The basic principles of construction are : a very shallow foundation (less than two feet at Kilmacduagh and Kilkenny) sometimes on an earlier burial site; an outer wall with a distinct batter, or tapering; an inner wall divided into several storeys with offsets to take the floors and one small window at each level; usually four stages; four windows in the topmost stage, the windows themselves tapering and following the incline of the outer skin; finally the conical roof with its capstone and cross.

Most important, the entrance doorway is placed as high up as possible, fifteen feet up in some cases, both to give strength to the base and to make it easier to repel intruders. Often from ground level to doorway the space was filled in with stone rubble, to give yet greater stability.

There are many examples with later work than those early Celtic simplicities and standard form. Battlements take the place of the conical roofcap; from the twelfth century a bell might be hung in the topmost level. There is a sprinkling of Romanesque doorway arches as at Dromiston, Co. Louth and Timahoe in Co. Laois, which is carved in four receding orders. At Scattery, on an island in the Shannon estuary near Kilrush, the doorway is at ground level. This tower may be very early, from a time before the advantages of a high doorway had been realised. Scattery has lost its outer conical cap, leaving only the rounded inner shell of the roof. This gives it a very odd look indeed.

One of the best known is at Ardmore, Co. Waterford. Excessively tapering, ninety-seven feet high with three elegant string courses, standing in lonely pride beside the seashore, this is twelfth century.

Apart from one in the Isle of Man and two in Scotland, all influenced by their Irish exemplars, the Round Towers are unique to Ireland.

The tower at Ardmore

Bramfield Church Tower, Suffolk

Is it too fanciful to suppose that the round towers of Norfolk and Suffolk, mostly within reach of the River Waveney which divides the counties, owe their inspiration to the Irish Round Towers? Certainly Scots from Ireland came early to the East Anglian shores, probably *via* Northumbria, that English centre of Celtic Christianity, and set up missions in rivalry to the great Pope Gregory's Roman Mission started by Augustine of Canterbury. Their headquarters is supposed to have been within the perimeter of Roman Burgh Castle, near Lowestoft. A nice irony.

More likely is the explanation that with the flint and ragstone available, a round tower rather than a square one was the easier shape to build something which would last. They certainly have lasted; their origin is firmly rooted in the eleventh century—pre-Norman— although all of them have survived because of later strengthening and embellishment.

Norfolk is their principal situation; the tower at Bramfield is chosen, not to annoy Norfolk friends, but because it is wholly detached from its delightful reed-thatched church by a distance of yards. This is unique, the nearest claimant being Little Snoring in Norfolk, but that is connected to the parent church by a covered passageway.

At Bramfield there are five bells, but they no longer ring. Their timbers in the bellchamber are unable to take the strain. The stone structure seems sound enough; the walls are very thick, about five feet in the ringing loft, with four little round arched unglazed air holes. On the deep embrasure of one of these stood a very tired pewter tankard and an empty bottle with moulded lettering proclaiming 'malt vinegar'. A likely story.

Inside the little church is a fine rood-screen, with some of its panelled paintings intact and agreeably restored.

In the chancel there are eighteenth-century stone slabs in the paving, with remarkable wording. Oddest of them is one to the memory of Bridgett Applethwaite, *née* Nelson: 'After the fatigues of Married Life born by her with incredible patience . . . and after the Enjoyment of the Glorious Freedom of an Easy and Unblemish'd Widowhood . . . she resolved to run the risk of a second Marriage Bed but DEATH forbad the Banns.'

The lengthy inscription goes on about her final terrible convulsions, plaintive groans or stupefying sleep. Without recovery of her speech or senses she 'dyed' in 1737. She lies flanked by Applethwaite relations, also with lengthy inscriptions.

It makes you wonder whether she, or the sympathetic scribe, had also had a go at the vinegar bottle.

Orford Castle, Suffolk

When Henry II attained the throne of England in 1154 there were no royal castles in East Anglia. He quickly confiscated the major strongholds in the hands of baronial magnates but handed back Framlingham and Bungay to the powerful Hugh Bigod, Earl of Norfolk, but not Thetford and Walton. In the same year Henry II began the building of Orford Castle, completing it in 1173 just in time to thwart a revolt supported by Earl Hugh and inspired by his own son Henry. The rebels laid siege to Orford but soon moved on, to their swift defeat.

Orford seems never to have been urgently needed as a royal bastion since then, and as early as 1336 Edward III granted it in perpetuity to the Earls of Suffolk. It remained in private hands until earlier this century.

The great polygonal keep, its three square towers jutting from a circular plan, was originally surrounded by outer defences of curtain walls and turrets, all now reduced to grassy mounds. From the modern flat roof just below the 90-foot topmost height, the view is like a map of the intricacies of the Alde and Ore estuaries, boats lying in the channels, the bird sanctuary of Havergate Island, Orford Ness lighthouse, 99-feet high, crowning a marshland nature reserve. To the north beyond Aldeburgh is Sizewell nuclear power station and below you the little town of Orford, with its fourteenth-century church tower, itself a considerable landmark.

The keep has been tactfully restored since it came under the care of the Department of the Environment, and so reverted to its original ownership by the Crown.

Orford has the human touches which give it the feel of a place where men lived. The chapel is recognisable by its round-arched arcading, aumbries, piscina and altar. There is a sink in the kitchen with an outflow through the thickness of the wall and four garderobes, or privies, whose chutes can be seen outside. Their stone seats are glass covered now, so that you can see down to daylight but do nothing else. There is even a pissoir for lighter relief. All these are placed at the end of angled passages, to minimise bad smells. One small chamber has a deep recess, or cupboard, possibly a repository for valuables.

There is only one official notice, on an easel in the lower circular hall, which reads :

'Any person writing on or scratching the fabric of this monument will be liable to prosecution'

This warning seems to be observed, although you can wander about at will with no guardians to watch you. In the keep there is no litter bin, and practically no litter.

Durham Cathedral

A train journey of occasional convenience to me starts with the Harwich boat train. The boat train from Harwich to Manchester. Once a day in each direction between these two ports, it passes Ely, its central octagon and west towers dominating miles of Fenland, to Peterborough. Get out here and wait for the London train to Newcastle, which soon comes in on a punctual day.

Then you can window shop past some more of England's noblest churches and many humble ones besides. Grantham, Newark, Retford, Doncaster, Selby, York, Durham and so to Newcastle, its crown almost lost amongst the view of Tyne bridges and tower blocks.

We get out at Durham, and go up the rocky backbone on which stand castle and Cathedral, intimately connected, for this was the centre of the County Palatine, a powerful form of early devolution. The eye is lifted up and caught by the central tower even as the eye fixes on it from the slowly moving train on its embankment.

On a foggy Sunday afternoon in winter between services there was nowhere so quiet as the massive Norman nave, most Norman of all the great cathedrals despite the extensions, alterations, destructions and fussing improvements which visited the place in later centuries since its curiously shallow foundations were laid in 1093.

In the Galilee Chapel which covers the west front lie the bones of the Venerable Bede; far away beyond the high altar is the shrine of St. Cuthbert, an even earlier saint and a cult figure of Northumbria, a shepherd boy from the Lammermuir Hills who saw a vision, became a bishop of Lindisfarne, was first buried there and later moved to Durham, a more impregnable fortress.

Marauding Scots never took it, though the Earls of Northumberland did in 1569, briefly, on behalf of Catholic Mary, Queen of Scots. In 1650, after the battle of Dunbar, several thousand prisoners from the defeated Scottish army were herded, cold and starving, into the cathedral by Cromwell's men. To keep warm they burnt precious carved stalls and the like.

Puritans had already done some smashing down of beauty and, later, those improvers James Wyatt, Anthony Salvin and Gilbert Scott got busy. None of them has succeeded in shifting the strong sense that this is a temple of pious, powerful Normans.

Get outside and look your fill at those towers; the two western towers rise 144 feet from the high rock. The central tower, perpendicular of the fifteenth century and yet aptly crowning it all, is dominant at 218 feet. It is not usually misty up there and with a wide prospect all round you can forget Wyatt and Salvin and Scott.

Norwich Cathedral

When Bishop Herbert de Losinga laid the foundations of the cathedral church of the Holy and Undivided Trinity on a low-lying site at Norwich in 1096, he and his masons can have had no idea that their successors would erect on their Norman lantern tower above the crossing an elegant spire pricking the sky to a height of 315 feet from the ground.

Work on the tower was quick but strong. By 1150 it had risen to the level below the present battlements. The tower has an inner and an outer skin, tied at intervals and with high narrow passages between. The present spire is the fourth, built in 1480.

Stand amazed at the cheek and the confidence of those who planned and carried out this work on top of a tower never meant to carry more than a squat pyramidal roof. That was the probable shape of the first spire, of wood, burnt down by riotous fellows in 1272. The second fell in a wind in 1362, the third was struck by lightning in 1463. Fourth time lucky; the 1480 spire has had in recent years extensive and skilful strengthening which has made as sure as can be that it will last, slender and thin walled (only 9 inches thick above the supporting buttresses), for centuries to come.

To climb up there is a sensation in itself, but there is no general access to those heights. I was a privileged mountaineer, accompanied by the cathedral's deputy architect, Mr. Keith Darby.

But do not just feast your eye on this eminence. The Norman lantern tower, the flying buttresses of the east end, or Presbytery, and the fan-vaulted ceiling within, as well as much else in a building which escaped the worst horrors of Victorian antiquarianism, are worth a close look. Even Mr. Anthony Salvin was kept in order when in 1833 he remodelled the South transept to match properly the original Norman of the North.

Norwich is proud—justly, but perhaps a little too proud—and the campanile of the City Hall, built in the 1930s at 202 feet on a higher site than the Cathedral, in a style borrowed from Ostberg's Town Hall in Stockholm, is no disgrace and no competitor to the Cathedral spire. Sweden is a bit out of the fashion now; perhaps that is a pity. Norwich set its own standards, long centuries ago, and these are what Norwich firmly believes in, despite the busy one-way traffic systems and some pretty dreadful shopping emporiums.

York Minster

Despite the warming effects of climbing the 275 steps to the parapet of the central tower of York Minster it was quickly chilly in the winter afternoon sunshine. The wide vista of the Plain of York and surrounding hills was reflected in the expanse of the newly restored roof of this wide tower, 69 foot square. Because of its massive area, its height of 197 feet is not apparent from below. In any case the pinnacled western towers rise 18 inches higher.

The present church was begun in 1220 by Walter de Gray, Archbishop from 1216 to 1255, who was appointed at the beginning of the even longer reign of Henry III. Building went on for over 250 years, culminating in the Perpendicular central tower, completed in 1480. It replaces an earlier tower which collapsed in a storm in 1407 and was meant to be topped by a steeple.

It is just as well this was never put up, for in 1966 it was found that the four piers on which the tower rests, each supporting 4000 tons of masonry and wood, were sinking unevenly into the ground. A mass of concrete and steel now reinforces the foundations, all a part of the extensive repairs of recent years to the whole fabric, now completed.

Within, all is shining bright and beautiful, including the lantern ceiling of the central tower, 185 feet above the paving. The best way to see this is to risk charges of irreverence and eccentricity and lie down on your back. The peal of 13 bells is housed in the South-west Tower; 'Big Peter' in the North-west. The dedication of the church is to St. Peter.

The curious visitor may care to notice a Roman column standing across the street from the south door. This was found during excavations in 1969 under the south transept floor. It had collapsed at that spot some 1600 years earlier and lain unnoticed. It honours a Roman legion stationed at Eboracum and was given to York Civic Trust by the Dean and Chapter.

Beverley Minster, some miles away, is considered by architectural purists the finer of the two. Certainly its twin West towers are outstanding, but to me the whole complex of York is the winner.

Top: York Minster
Bottom: Beverley Minster

Caerphilly Castle, Mid-Glamorgan
Kidwelly Castle, Dyfed

Wales is so much a land of castles that to choose only a few of them is to invite the scorn of knowing persons. Nearly all of them in their present form show that they were built not by the Welsh for Wales but by the English against the Welsh. From the Conquest onwards waves of strongholds from which to Normanise the wild land were being built.

Edward I brought the process to a climax. He built and rebuilt and took over castles all over Wales and the Welsh Marshes. His unsatisfactory son Edward II was born at Caernarvon and in 1301 created Prince of Wales. The Principality was now deemed to have been conquered; the Red Dragon and those famous feathers were added to the emblems of the English Royal House.

Caerphilly, or Caerffili, is not far out of Cardiff. Drive over the Caerphilly Mountain and you see the town and this immense stronghold below you in a wide bowl of hills. Thirty acres of stone and water. It was built in the thirteenth century by Gilbert de Clare, a Marcher lord, and was the first medieval fortress in Britain to have concentric rings of defence. Edward I was so impressed that he adopted the system for the Tower of London, where this pattern of protection can also be seen today.

Despite the scholarly and loving restoration of Caerphilly carried out within the past hundred years by the 3rd and 4th Marquesses of Bute, to me the place lacks feeling, is oppressive through sheer size. Too many walls and towers, one of them leaning dangerously and broken, a vast tooth suffering badly from caries.

Very different is my impression of Kidwelly, in Welsh Cydweli, so that there is no need to try to pronounce the name of either castle as though you were rushing saliva through your back teeth.

An artist friend drove me to this castle commanding Carmarthen Bay. It is known that building began within 50 years of the Norman Conquest. Most of what we see at Kidwelly today dates from 1275 and building went on right through the 14th century and later.

Dates do not matter where atmosphere is strong. The artist's heightened perception of the colour and form of stone—a favourite theme of her work—and a shared sense of the *genius loci*, lit up these ruins for us on a grey day with a quality that sunlight could not have done.

The artist drove me back to Cardiff *via* the mountain road. In the rain, visible on a high ridge above the River Tywi, she pointed out to me Paxton's Tower, a folly built in 1811 to Samuel Pepys Cockerell's design for the landowner, Sir William Paxton. It is also a monument to Nelson.

Top: Caerphilly Castle
Centre: Kidwelly Castle
Bottom: Paxton's Tower, before its restoration
by the National Trust

Conwy Castle, Gwynedd
Harlech Castle, Gwynedd

The big four castles of the sea approaches to North Wales were Conwy, Caernarvon, Harlech and Beaumaris. In each case Edward I and his architect from Savoy, James of St George, were responsible for the palace fortresses of which we see the remains today.

Conwy was the site of Llywelyn the Great's palace, and he was buried there. Edward I changed all that, and built this massive castle with its eight towers so marvellously disposed with symmetry as to look as neat as—what, a cake? Certainly not; much more, to borrow the phrase from the late Barbara Jones, like 'a tiara of castellations'. Great walls on its rocky elevation link them and there is, besides, the town wall projecting northwards.

Already there was a town here, now linked across the tidal estuary by three bridges, one for rail, one for road and one for footwear. Today the little town is busy and besieged by traffic. It brings many visitors and the demand for a relieving bypass. Which will win, the traffic or the towers and walls? This is a town castle and the restorations that began in the nineteenth century—even the railway company joined in the work —still go on. All paths and stairs and walkways to which there is access are concrete smooth. The work has not obliterated the number of arrow slits and other points from which to draw a bow. It bristles and could be held by very few men. It is a beautiful place, and specially vulnerable to the pressures of today.

Harlech, too, was capable of defence by a very small garrison. Originally the sea lapped the steep scarp it stands on, but the sea and Tremadoc Bay have retreated. From the outer walls you see not only the steep steps down to the watergate, there is also a splendid view of a housing estate and a caravan site, with the sand dunes a mile away.

Edward I made a great stronghold here between 1285 and 1290, but the name most associated with Harlech is Owain Glyn Dwr, or Glendower. In 1404 Glyn Dwr took it and held it for the Welsh for four years.

On a fine day the cold west wind blew holes through stout clothing, both at Conwy and at Harlech. On the road between them, through a Snowdonian defile, stands Dolwyddelan Castle, birthplace of Llywelyn the Great, built by his father and rebuilt by Edward I, the perpetual castle builder. Lonely on a crag, all that is seen from the road is the peel tower.

Of the three Conwy is the most picturesque, Harlech the most imposing, with two ranges of gatetowers and enormous towers at each corner of the inner ward. Dolwyddelan looks the most tragic, glooming without pity for itself or anybody.

Top: Conwy Castle
Centre: Harlech Castle
Bottom: Dolwyddelan Castle

Salisbury Cathedral

The proportions of Salisbury Cathedral are so exact that it is difficult to realise that here is our highest spire, our Number One at 404 feet. It also has the quality, unique amongst our ancient cathedrals, of its principal interior being built all of a piece, the nave and the two transept crossings—the double cross—complete by the early years of the thirteenth century in the style known, and joked about by those who like to tease art historians as Early English or E.E.

Many years ago I took a very volatile Cockney friend to see this church. Going in at the North door I distracted his attention towards the tall triple window of the West front until we reached the halfway point. Then I switched him round to face East. 'Oh! my Gawd. Don't it make you think of 'eaven?' He was beholding the whole length, 449 feet, to the East Window.

The style is too severe for my taste : the clustered columns of pale Chilmark limestone emphasised by incorporating slender shafts of black Purbeck marble; repeated along the triforium gallery; elevating once more to frame the clerestory and ultimately to support the ribs of the roof.

Despite the apparent unity, Wren in his time was called in to advise on repairs. In the eighteenth century James Wyatt took things away; Gilbert Scott put some back in the nineteenth.

Now for the crowning glory. The original summit was only just above the roofs of nave and crossing. Mark the first horizontal course of the tower held on corbelled brackets. Later came the rest of the tower, and the spire was completed in 1365.

The most comfortable place to look at this from a near point is in the cloisters. They are behind the great wall stretching southward from the West front. Notice its scale—the black dot in the picture is a woman.

In the centre of the perfect square of the cloisters are two cedar trees. Lean back against one of the buttresses of the cloister arcade at a point where the cedars can be seen only to give scale to your upward gaze at the steeple. In that posture there is no tendency to get giddy.

On the day of my visit the winter snows had at last gone; there was blue sky and quick white clouds. For a long time I leant and looked at the still spire and the passing pageant of white flock behind it. I, too, thought of Heaven.

Coming back to earth I escaped into the big spread of flat mown lawn bordered by the elegant buildings of the Cathedral Close. A very open Close. Seeing people passing in and out of their houses, I wondered whether they could possibly be ordinary sinful mortals when they have always this great sight before them.

Stock, Essex

There is, in the southern part of Essex, a fairly close grouping of wooden church towers and steeples, all easy of access from Chelmsford. As a spectacle, the queen of them is All Saints at Stock, a pleasant, open village. All Saints was constructed of oak timbers between 1250 and 1300, so the scholars say, and from the date 1683 carved on the north face of the tower it is probable that the vertical oak boards of the square base were then renewed. The shingles of the steeple are a recent renewal.

These belfries are ingeniously contrived, the wide eaves dropping off rainwater well clear of the walls. They are very strong—the interior timbers are massive and need to be to resist wind and take the strain of swinging bells—and at Stock the impression of gracefulness outside is conveyed by the white paint of the belfry and the slim steeple. Church and old and new rectory are set in a glebe now cut as a lawn throughout.

An eighteenth-century rector, the Rev. William Unwin, was friend and protector of the poet William Cowper, whose bouts of melancholia sometimes took him to the point of madness. He first lived with the Unwins at Huntingdon, and he must have visited them at Stock, for one of his poems is entitled 'The Yearly Distress or Tithing Time at Stock':

> This priest he merry is and blithe
> Three quarters of the year,
> But Oh! it cuts him like a scythe
> When tithing time draws near.
>
> For then the farmers come jog, jog,
> Along the miry road,
> Each heart as heavy as a log,
> To make their payments good.
>
> In sooth, the sorrow of such days
> Is not to be express'd,
> When he that takes and he that pays
> Are both alike distress'd.
>
> Now all unwelcome, at his gates
> The clumsy swains alight,
> With rueful faces and bald pates—
> He trembles at the sight.
>
> And well he may, for well he knows
> Each bumpkin of the clan,
> Instead of paying what he owes,
> Will cheat him if he can.

All that sorrow and rue and cheating is over now, though the Tithe War of the 1930s is not so very long ago.

When I first saw Stock it was at once familiar to me because of the many board and shingled steeples in my native Kent, not forgetting the strange object tucked away at Brookland on Romney Marsh, where there sits in the churchyard a belfry quite detached from its church, looking like three great wooden dunce's caps stacked one upon another. It is sometimes classed as a folly. No wonder.

St. Mary & All Saints, Chesterfield, Derbyshire

Look at it from which way you will, it twists and turns from every angle. Approached from the north east, across a narrow valley, it stands up prominently, for Chesterfield is centred on a ridge and the spire itself rises 228 feet from the base of the tower. It was completed before 1400, and the great puzzle is whether it was given this twist on purpose—the herring-bone pattern of the lead claddings emphasises it—or whether green timber was used and split and twisted in the course of time? The unusual dedication to St. Mary & All Saints can have nothing to do with it.

The effect of the leading is an illusion, that the spire has eight channelled ribs, but this is not the case. The two halves of each herring-bone face are quite flat in relation to one another. It is one of the mysteries, as well as one of the principal curiosities, of English church building.

Within the body of the church there is a confusing display of marvels, though the nave is sturdy nineteenth-century, restored and decorated Gothic. There are the sixteenth-century Foljambe tombs in alabaster and marble, a medieval rood-screen, a fine Jacobean pulpit, eighteenth-century brass candelabra, and a welter of nineteenth-century and later embellishments started by Gilbert Scott in 1843. This church has long been a shrine of the High Anglican party, and none the worse for that. Sir Ninian Comper worked here.

Sadly, it must be reported that in Chesterfield it is not only the spire that is twisted. A cleaner with whom I was talking noticed a young couple who, she was sure, were trying to unscrew the wall plates with coin slots for offerings and payments for literature. 'You can't get money out of there' she told them in the sturdy voice of a Derbyshire matron, 'You'd better be going'. She turned to me. 'They've been hanging about for an hour. They saw you put money in. A month ago my purse was stolen and now I have to take my bag round wherever I'm working. Cigarette butts I've found up there in the Chapel, and other things besides.' I thought of the No Smoking signs in the church at Stoke-by-Nayland in Suffolk where artistic brass rubbing can be done for a fee, and was not surprised. The signs are now removed, but the rubbing goes on.

Bell Harry Tower,
Canterbury Cathedral

The Pilgrim's Way, cutting along under the skirt of the
Kentish North Downs, is a modern misnomer for an
ancient Neolithic track leading to the place now called
Canterbury. Devout pilgrims to the Cathedral in which
St. Thomas Becket was murdered may have used it,
but the proper way for the pilgrims from the west was
along Roman Watling Street, the route taken by
Chaucer's tale-telling travellers.

A number of years ago—I will not announce the
date—a man drove his daughter dressed in white to her
confirmation at Canterbury along the same road. In
those days the traffic-tangled Medway towns had to
be got through, and here we must pause a moment, for
the Norman keep of Rochester Castle rises 104 feet and
the conical spire on the apparently squat tower of the
Cathedral 156 feet. After this hazard there is the
succession of villages set in orchards—Bapchild,
Ospringe, Boughton Street, Dunkirk. The young girl
became a little drowsy and then, over the hump at
Harbledown, she saw a magnificent sight.

'What is that big church over there?'

'Canterbury Cathedral, darling, that is where you are
going.'

It is not as if this were her first glimpse of Canterbury. We often passed through it on our way to holidays at Westgate-on-Sea and there was also the
obligatory outing to Canterbury Cricket Week, to St.
Laurence's Ground where a friendly little train would
pass to and fro on an embankment. What my sister saw
was the great central tower of the Cathedral, the 'Bell
Harry'.

It is of much later date than the main body of the
church, being built between 1495 and 1517. It is the
work of John Wastell who also had a part in the building of King's College Chapel at Cambridge. It is not
only a thing of beauty as a whole; the detail is superb
and, with fewer stages than Gloucester, those elongated
perpendicular windows carry it to a height of 235 feet.

Centuries of pilgrims have flocked to Canterbury,
especially since the martyrdom of St. Thomas, canonised
in 1173, long before the Bell Harry Tower was built.
Their ardour may have cooled somewhat after the
Reformation. One of the more notable of the early
stained glass windows, dating from the 13th century,
depicts the martyrdom.

The Tower is known as the Bell Harry because that
is the name of the one bell in an earlier tower, not
because of any King Henry. There is no public admis-
sion to its heights.

Warkworth Castle, Northumberland

Uninhabited and partly ruinous, Warkworth Castle, hanging above its attendant village and the River Coquet, is a fine example of a fourteenth-century fortress which was also a roomy residence. There had been a castle here for centuries by the time it came into the hands of the Percy family in 1332. By the end of the fourteenth century the Earl of Northumberland (Hotspur's father in Henry IV Part One) had run up the tower-like keep which remains its dominant feature today. The outer defences are still standing to show not only the great strength of the place but also its comfort, with their storage chambers for victuals and the like within the central enclosure.

Northumberland, Cumbria and the Border country in Scotland are studded with meaningful castles and keeps and peel towers. They were necessary. Never from earliest times a peaceful region, a consequence of Edward I's attempts to subdue Scotland was to increase the wild lawlessness of the border dales on both sides of the divide in the centuries after his death in 1307. Families of great, or even little, property, tried defensively to protect themselves from their neighbours as much as to aid the realm.

Raiding for horses and cattle in a country impoverished, as is usually the way, by the need for a strong military presence, made the country yet poorer and more lawless. So the vicious circle was by force completed and made more vicious by the habit of clever kings in ordering their commanders to let slip bands of professional, not part-time, raiders upon the enemy of the day. 'Limmer' thieves they were called.

Warkworth is only one example of a major bastion of a great family. There are many such on both sides of the border.

Smailholm Tower, Roxburgh

At the opposite end of the scale of grandeur from Warkworth Castle and its like, the Peel Tower of Smailholm, lonely on its crag 900 feet above sea level, stands like a broken sentinel. The place is harshly romantic, as Sir Walter Scott well recognised. Protected by rocks from which the remains of its outer defences emerge, with water on one side and walls 9 feet thick, it must have been a challenge.

In the dangerous centuries it was in the hands of the family of Pringle, or Hop-Pringle, who were there by 1453. They were sureties for the ransom of a more important man taken prisoner by the English at the Battle of Pinkie in 1547—a period of official war known as the Rough Wooing which made use of the perpetual private feuding and raiding—and later the harrying by the English became so intense that John Hop-Pringle joined the English, in common with many lesser lairds who had few friends and many enemies.

One of my great-great-grandmothers was a Pringle from this part of Scotland and I like to think her ancestors held Smailholm. And if they changed sides, who am I to blame them?

At this time not only the gentry but even the priests needed protection and on both sides of the Border there are Vicar's Peles—you can spell the word which way you like—and these were refuges for the holy men.

In dreadful contrast to them and to Smailholm, Hermitage stands on the damp, misty moors above Liddesdale, a principal source of generations of 'limmers'. Never call Hermitage a castle; it was a prison from which there was little chance of escape. A forerunner of Dartmoor, its square mass of masonry now has a certain elegance.

Despite Sir Walter Scott's affection for it, I doubt if Hermitage has had many suitors, but everybody who sees Smailholm falls for it. Lord Home of the Hirsel—whose ancestors played a large part in the turbulence of those ancient days—tells a story of being taken as a boy to the rocky hill on which Smailholm stands the better to see the passing of early aeronauts in the Daily Mail Round Britain air race. Aeroplanes named after Blériot took part and the race was won by 'Beaumont', the pseudonym of a lieutenant of the French navy.

In the closing weeks of 1978 Smailholm was in splints undergoing extensive renovation following damage from gales to its top. Like Hermitage, it is in the care of the Ancient Monuments Board for Scotland.

Top: Smailholm
Bottom: Hermitage

Borthwick Castle, Lothian

Leave the Galashiels road some twelve miles south of Edinburgh, take a small road down an incline, round a bend towards a small valley and there stands the commanding and impressive bulk of Borthwick Castle. It fills the landscape, standing on a steep bank above the confluence of two burns, almost obliterating the village cluster below it. Built in 1430 for the lords of Borthwick, it is two massive peel towers joined together, over 100 feet high, and leaving a gulf between them known as the prisoners' leap. In a place like this, myth and reality need not be reconciled.

At the base the walls are 20 feet thick, 10 to 14 feet quite high up, and it is calculated that the weight of stone used in its building exceeds 30,000 tons. There are no gun loops; in that house the possibility of attack was not considered. But there were, and still are, gun ports at the base of one of the perimeter walls. Cromwell knocked it about a bit; the scars of his cannon fire, high up, can still be seen.

House as well as fortress indeed it is, and always was, with an astonishing array of great chambers and smaller chambers all within the thick walls of the original fifteenth-century plan. This has not been altered since its first building, though two phases of restoration are evident.

Left unoccupied for two centuries until the turn of the present century, even the ceilings and floors were of stone, and so fireproof, though at this first restoration some wooden floors and ceilings were introduced. It became again a Borthwick property and now has in Miss Helen Bailey a life tenant whose recent restoration and fitting out won a European Heritage Year Award in 1975.

Let us now go back to the sixteenth century. Lord Borthwick adhered to Mary, Queen of Scots, who often visited the castle. Her husband Bothwell's Crichton Castle is only two or three miles away. When the tide was running strongly against them in 1567, they went to Borthwick from Edinburgh. Their enemies pursued them. Bothwell fled and Mary, so the story goes, slipped out to join him disguised as a page. A few days later Bothwell was defeated at Carberry Hill and this was the end of Mary's fragile freedom and power.

From the roof there is a panorama of the Pentland Hills to the west and Crichton Castle, a tidied-up ruin, can be easily seen to the north east. The prisoners' leap is a frightening chasm. A man could gain his freedom by jumping across with his hands tied. Failure seems to me certain even to the most powerful long jumper; refusal to try probably meant a slower and even more horrible death.

Gloucester Cathedral

The sky was blue, the air nippy. Approaching Gloucester from the south along the road superseded by a motorway running parallel, the great tower sparkled in its elaborate face of hard Painswick lime-stone, recently cleaned. In the inner city it disappeared save for an occasional glimpse. The most dramatic approach on foot is to walk along Westgate Street, turn into the alley called College Court, and there you are on College Green facing the south door and the central tower in marvellous isolation, for there are no west towers at Gloucester.

Looking at the entire edifice from the outside, with the ingeniously wrought Gothic tracery and spacious windows, it is difficult to realise that this is still basically a Norman Abbey Church. The fat and lofty cylinders and round arches of the nave are unmistakeable. Surrounding them is the lighter, later work. In the choir there is a curious reversal. Framed within apparently squat Norman pillars is a masterpiece of early perpendicular fourteenth century. Beyond that, beyond the Presbytery, is the vast space of the East window, the Crecy window.

There is much history of kings at Gloucester. The boy King Henry III was crowned here in 1216. Here stands the elaborate tomb of Edward II, murdered at Berkeley Castle nearby in 1327, put up by his son Edward III. Richard II held a Parliament here in 1378. London was hostile and unsafe for his advisers.

'Gloucester' said a friend, 'Yes, one of England's glories'. I go along with that. A guidebook quoted some source saying that it was the sixth best church in Europe. How can anybody objectively arrive at such a silly judgment? The birthplace of the peculiarly English Perpendicular style is another claim.

There was no chance of climbing that day; the work of rehanging the bells and improving access for the bellringers was still going on. Nor was there any wish to climb. That part of England is full of stupendous views from natural heights and Gloucester is in the plain of the Severn, below the Cotswolds and its out-lying scarps.

I went outside to College Green, and did not hear Big Peter, the only remaining medieval great bell, or bourdon, in England. Forgetting all the dazzling remarks, I looked up. Above the successive stages of pointed arches the motif suddenly changes. The high pierced parapet and the pierced corner turrets and pinnacles are so delicate, like a crown. Built between 1450 and 1460, it rises 225 feet from the ground, on sure Norman foundations.

I went on looking, and looking, at blue sky through stone tracery. After a harsh winter there seemed even better things to contemplate than the prospect of spring.

St. Michael's, Glastonbury Tor, Somerset

John Crow, a louche and sexy sponger in Paris, returns to his native Norfolk to attend his grandfather's funeral, to Northwold, where the River Wissey wanders down from Brandon Heath to the marshlands of Norfolk. He has no expectations. On the way to the obsequies he meets his cousin Mary, another Crow. They immediately engage in his chosen, equivocal kind of coupling.

She, the virginal and penniless companion of Miss Euphemia Drew of Glastonbury, is not surprised, only delighted. They are late for the funeral. This threadbare scarecrow announces his intention of walking to Glastonbury; their rich cousin Philip, who owns a factory there, will employ him. Mary empties her slender purse into his hand and he sets off. He stops at Stonehenge, at his last gasp, and is lifted the rest of the way in the car of Owen Evans, who also lives in Glastonbury. A dangerous man full of Cymric lore and obsessed by the perverted lust of a killing blow delivered by an iron bar.

As they approach the Isle of Avalon John Crow 'became aware of the dim pyramidal form of Glastonbury Tor, towering above the walls and roofs of the town. As soon as he caught sight of this great pointed hill, with the massive deserted church tower on its summit, he felt conscious that here was something that suited his nature . . . ' Mr Evans murmurs something about St. Michael the Archangel. Crow thought: 'To hell with St. Michael. That Tower is nothing but a tall pile of stones. I like that Tower—I shall go up that Tower at the first chance.'

This is the begining of the immense Manichaean saga by J. C. Powys oddly named *A Glastonbury Romance*, one of the great novels of our age. I can never approach Glastonbury, especially with that view of St. Michael's sitting atop what seems to be a huge burial mound, without being reminded of that book and its many curiosities.

Alas! the Tower, only a shell, is architecturally undistinguished, but is set 500 feet on the Tor commanding an immense view to the Mendips in the north, the Polden Hills to the south, and all round the marshy moors low lying beside the River Brue. It is coarse Perpendicular in style, with an earlier west door, and the chapel it announces has long since disappeared.

When I first read *A Glastonbury Romance* I had early assumed that John Crow was certain to come to a sticky end; but no, he turns out to be a precarious survivor. Let us hope that the Archangel's Tower on Glastonbury Tor will more certainly survive.

Cromer Church, Norfolk

Approaching from Norwich the road bends and traces a mild downward slope through the environs of the small seaside town of Cromer. Bang in the middle of this somewhat smug view the great tower of St. Peter and St. Paul hits the eye. At 160 feet it is East Anglia's highest, early fifteenth-century Perpendicular. The church itself is heavily Victorianised, due to neglect almost to the point of ruin in the eighteenth century and earlier, but notice the very high arch framing the interior of the tower.

Necessary restoration of the tower was done in 1885, and since then the turret stairs have been thoroughly repaired. The pairs of bell-chamber windows are set on all four sides and the square air holes in the ringing loft, often found in Norfolk churches, have a rich geometric pattern. In the sea-facing northern air hole lanterns were once placed to serve as a beacon to seafarers. Many east coast church towers served this purpose.

Aloft, parapet and pinnacles are richly crocketed. Apart from these, and the stone dressing of the buttresses, all is of knapped flint, with no flushwork.

Not far from Cromer are the beautiful halls of Blickling and Felbrigg, both seventeenth century and both National Trust properties. As for neighbouring church towers, there are

'Gimingham, Trimingham, Knapton and Trunch
Northrepps and Southrepps — all in a bunch'.

Tattershall Castle, Lincolnshire

Created by one powerful statesman in the mid-fifteenth century, when the unhappy years of the Wars of the Roses were brewing trouble for everyone; restored by another statesman of eminence just before World War I, Tattershall Castle is a monument to its builder, Ralph, Lord Cromwell, Treasurer of England under Henry VI, and to its restorer George Nathaniel, Marquess Curzon of Kedleston, who failed to become leader of the Conservative Party, which he ardently wished to be.

Built of red brick, the great keep stands on the stone foundations of an earlier castle, which you can see in the deeps of the once water-filled moat. Four great turrets, rising over 100 feet, appear to guard an impressive rectangle which piles one above another four great central chambers with generous arched windows and massive fireplaces. Small rooms in the turrets lead off these halls, and still smaller ones within the thickness of the walls.

This was built not as a defensive stronghold, though perhaps to frighten off intruders, but to crown the many possessions of Ralph Cromwell, who inherited riches and married an heiress. She was a Deincourt, a significant name in Tennyson's county. Once, that red brick was washed over with a violent rouge de terre or red ochre. That would certainly frighten off adherents of today's horrid Suffolk Pink.

For Ralph Cromwell the Middle Ages were over; he was in advance of the Tudor period of theatrical magnificence but he was showing those successors how to do it. Within, look at the four great chimneypieces—the best of them in the ground-floor parlour—and the moulded brick arches of the windows. Above the Parlour is the seigneurial hall, above that the audience chamber, and on the fourth level the private chamber. Crowning all, above the machicolations, an arcaded roof walk and even higher turrets.

From every point of the roof there is a magnificent view of land and sky and water. In this flat land, from that height the elements seem to merge into one another. At ground level all is flat, and tidy, save for the picturesque moat growing elegant reeds. There is, also, the fine collegiate church adjoining. Cromwell built the castle for show and the church for the good of his soul. Curzon restored for love.

He bought it in 1911, bought back the chimney-pieces from dealers, dug out the moat where other important masonry had been chucked, put architect and builders to work. There was a considerable political row about this, which led to the passing of the first Ancient Monuments Act of 1915. On his death in 1925 Curzon left it to the National Trust.

It is too perfect. The beautifully repointed brickwork outside and in, the smoothing up of the stone treads of the newel stair, the real but unused logs in the fires, petrify the place. It is as though Lutyens had built

here and gone away without putting in his heavy
oaken panelling. There is no sensation that anybody
lived here, so unlike the feeling you get at Orford. The
deadened feeling is accentuated by the sparse furnishing
of one or two rooms behind padlocked bars. In one of
the great chambers is a refectory table about the length
of a railway coach.

As I went towards Tattershall a drizzle replaced the
pale autumn sun. I drove in towards the car park as the
drizzle turned to rods of rain. I stopped where I should
not have done, just before the rustic wooden bridge of
the outer moat, facing the keep. Through the water
pouring across the curved windscreen the castle seemed
to shimmer and waver and shimmy. This was my best
view of it, and of course I knew it was really standing
unmoved by this small tempest. Even the chutes of the
invisible latrines have been converted into rainwater
run offs.

To me, more evocative and moving than the castle
itself are the names of places round about in that strange
flat land, marred as it is by pylons and poles : Holland
Fen and Dowsby Fen, Tumby Woodside and Marsham-
le-Fen, Frithville and Revesby, North Kyme and South
Kyme, Dogdyke and New York, Carrington and
Swineshead.

Boston Stump, Lincolnshire

Rising from 30 feet of alluvial silt beside the tidal Boston Haven, the builders of St. Botolph's were taking almighty risks in creating here England's largest parish church. All its dimensions are vast, and it has great beauty despite Puritan smashing down, and aided by sensitive restorations through to the present century. We are here concerned only with its great tower, known throughout the world by the name given to it by the friendly English Bostonians, who are not given to swank : 'Boston Stump'. It rises 272 feet from ground level, its foundations firmly in the hard clay below the silt, below even the bed of the river which laps it.

The Stump was not built all of a piece. It took nearly a century to complete, starting in 1430. Its crowning glory, the lantern, was built in the early sixteenth century, and its shell-thin walls are supported by flying buttresses. There could be no conical roof to cap such a delicate structure.

The lowest stage of 85 feet is held to be the work of Reginald of Ely, the first architect of King's College Chapel, Cambridge. Above the second stage, with its huge windows surmounted by the principal viewing balconies, is the belfry. The louvres for the ring of ten bells can be seen in the lower half of the windows of the third stage. The bells are supported on a reinforced concrete floor, and below this the ringers stand round the humped ceiling casing over the vaulted interior of the tower.

This ceiling was designed by George Place in 1853 and rises 137 feet above the paved floor within the church. Guard against giddiness when you look up. There is also a carillon of 15 bells, played by remote control from the library above the porch. Up the newel staircase leading to the galleries and the belfry can be seen iron collars to give support to the walls. These and the concrete floors with their reinforcement, help to tie in the precarious structure, which yet conveys such a sense of certainty.

This is dead flat country, and even from the first balcony, 145 feet up, it is claimed that on a clear day the towers of Lincoln can be seen in one direction and the Norfolk coast beyond The Wash in the other. Think of the view to be had by the happy men who in 1910 replaced one of the lantern pinnacles which, struck by lightning, had fallen through the church roof.

On the morning of my visit the military were briskly preparing arrangements for the funeral of a young soldier, a boy of eighteen, who had been killed in a road smash a few days earlier.

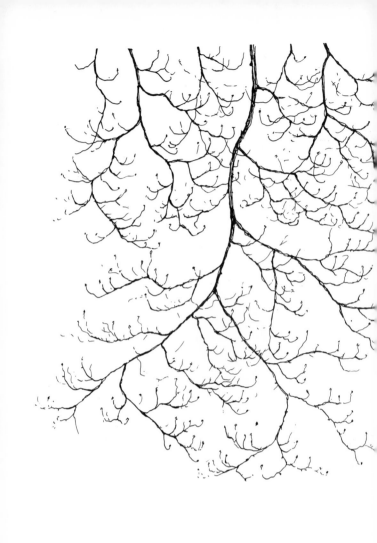

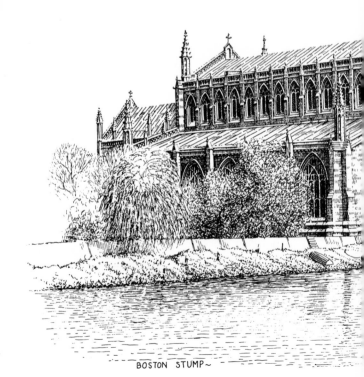

BOSTON STUMP~

JOHN BANGAY 78'

Magdalen Tower, Oxford

The retired warden of All Souls' College, Oxford, went to Chicago to perform there some intellectual exercises. On his return he talked about his experiences on Radio 3. If you want to see Magdalen Tower, he seemed to be saying, you must go to Chicago University where many Gothic splendours include a copy of it. It was no good looking at the original; it was practically down to the ground.

John Sparrow may have exaggerated; I may have misheard, but alarm bells rang in my mind and telephone calls were made. 'No—yes—extensive restoration —scaffolding—the structure sound—completion due in 1982. *It will be all right.*'

Magdalen Tower, 148 feet to the top of its pinnacles, was begun before 1500 when Wolsey was Bursar. The future Cardinal probably gave it an upward shove and it was completed in 1509. Mottled by the use of different stone from Headington, Forest Hill, Cleeve and elsewhere, and with the slight narrowing at each horizontal string course, the lower stages are plain. Then come the great windows of the top stage and above them the whole thing breaks into flower. The sub-parapet with quatrefoil ornament, the tall parapet above perforated, the turrets ending in a flourish of crocketed spirelets.

Between these corner turrets are median pinnacles, very slim, which continue upwards the line of the buttressing between the great windows. Slender as they are, there are niches with statues in them. Much of the stone and the carving had decayed and earlier synthetic restorations had developed hair cracks which let in the water. A gargoyle head weighing a quarter ton might drop off on the head of an innocent pedestrian or a Morris Minor. The work had to be done.

The 33rd President of Magdalen and the College Surveyor told me much and showed me much. The original plans did not exist, so working drawings of every course were made, and drawings of every carving, even though some of them are conjecture such was the extent of the decay. The skill, the care and the devotion being applied are awesome.

Before the coming of the railway and much else the principal entrance to Oxford was over Magdalen Bridge, and there was the Tower to greet the traveller. Not a dreaming spire in sight. For pleasure take the B480 road at the end of the Fair Mile out of Henley and follow it all the way to Magdalen Bridge. It passes through Cowley, all part of Our Heritage, and a small price to pay for the delights of a secondary road which was once a great highway.

When Charles I made Oxford his H.Q. after the Battle of Edgehill, stones were carried up the Tower with which to shower unwelcome visitors. When the present work is done, there should be little fear of dropping masonry for centuries. Not, at least, by accident.

St. Mary's, Totnes, Devon

In the autumn of 1936, the annual conference of the Council for the Protection of Rural England was held at Torquay. This was the beginning of my working for the London headquarters of that worthy body. When it was over I pleaded an excuse from my new employer to spend two days at Totnes. It was going to be the start of a Great Romance. I was wrong, but we are still friends in a distant sort of way.

To me, Totnes is one of the beautiful towns of England. Placed between the solemnities of Dartmoor and the splendours and miseries of the south Devon coast, it must be a favourite escape inland for those on holiday at Torquay and Paignton. Its centre is a narrow straight street which climbs like a spine up a hillside set in a bowl of higher hills, with the River Dart below and part of it. At about shoulder-blade point, there rises the tower of the church of St. Mary's, all in red sandstone with grey stone embellishments.

Stand, if passing tourists and shoppers allow, on the pavement opposite the South porch and look up at this West tower. It rises, firmly planted in the ground, like the fluting of great organ pipes. On each flank are buttresses rising to turrets; in the centre is the median tower, half an octagon, of the newel stair, which culminates in a turret with battlements, higher than the parapet. At this highest point the red all gives way to grey; battlements and corner turret pinnacles are in Beer or Portland stone. It is suspected that these topmost flights are 19th century improvements advised by Sir Gilbert Scott. Whatever their origin it is very pretty. Notice, just below the string course halfway up, the three niches with statues, capped above the horizontal course with their own little grey turrets and pinnacles. This is an unusual feature in the area, and is borrowed from Somerset.

The projecting stair turret is not so unusual. J. E. Morris, learned in these matters, counted 58 churches in the south-west likewise adorned, especially in this South Hams district centred on Totnes. They are not found in other parts of England. There is one at Wellington, in Somerset, of the same red sandstone. Above Wellington, above Wrangway, on the Blackdown Hills, stands the noble obelisk to the Great Duke. But we do not come to Totnes to celebrate soldiering.

Down river from Totnes comes the tidal estuary of the Dart, with Dartmouth Naval College almost at its mouth. Up river are the cultural excellencies of Dartington Hall and not far away, the twentieth-century rebuilding of the Benedictine Abbey of Buckfast, built by a few monks inspired by their Belgian Father Superior. Three different worlds.

When I went to Buckfast in 1936 it was still building. The tower of the Abbey church rises 158 feet, in the style known as Transitional, halfway between Norman and E.E.

Totnes church was all built in the mid-fifteenth century, but the interior is sadly Victorianised after earlier messing about with unsuitable galleries. There still remains a glorious screen and parclose, of carved stone, not wood, and with traces of vermilion and gilt which do not look original to my unschooled eye.

From the parapet of the tower I looked down on the antique roofs of the town, an experience denied to a crowd. It may be worth explaining why so many church and bell towers are not generally accessible. Here, the treads as far as the ringing loft (eight bells) are modern, of wood. The higher spiral to the parapet has the old stone treads, some of them worn to a tricky slope. No church can take responsibility for accidents going up and down these dark and difficult places. The church is for mending souls, not breaking bones.

At Totnes there is compensation, for the castle walls at the highest point of the town are free for use by those prepared to pay the modest charges of the Ancient Monuments Board. The walls are at a point even higher than the parapet of the church tower, but the prospect is wider, not so intimate as that which I enjoyed, where I could see how seventeenth- and eighteenth-century façades are fitted to the front of buildings much older.

Dundry Church, Avon

To the south of Bristol there is a long whaleback, steep-sided, running east and west. This is Dundry Hill, rising to nearly 800 feet. Near the summit is Dundry village, originally a quarry settlement. Its excellent stone is a principal ingredient of the great Bristol church of St. Mary Redcliffe. The stone is not worked now and it is sad to report that when I visited the top of the down, to the west of the church, it was a smoking rubbish dump. Let this please be a temporary beastliness.

Greater Bristol laps the northern shore of the hill and, in order to avoid picking through a tangle of streets, a rural, eastern approach was chosen. Steep banked muddy lanes demonstrated busy farming. The blackest of black clouds loomed to the west. So it had to be raining. Yet again? Luck, and lunch at one of the two inns on this perch, and a day of quick shifts, helped me in sunshine to this extraordinary church tower with the whole of Bristol and Avonmouth spread out below.

The church itself is very modest and almost entirely a Victorian rebuilding. The tower, nearly 100 feet high, is remarkable, almost unaltered Perpendicular dated 1482. The four lower stages are quite plain, many buttressed, most of the windows below the bellchamber being blind. The buttressing ceases before reaching the cornice of the parapet, which sits on the tower like a great square hat that is of a quite different character from the head and shoulders it rests on. The high parapet and the projecting corner turrets are pierced—a reminiscence of Gloucester—and each of the four pinnacles has its own weathervane.

It has been thought that Bristol merchants built the tower as an aid to shipping coming up the Bristol Channel into the Avon, but the Society of Merchant Venturers of Bristol was not incorporated until 1552. The records of an earlier Fellowship of Merchants do not exist for the period when Dundry was built. Perhaps individual merchants contributed. A note in the church states that the tower once had a lantern to act as a beacon for shipping.

The church is kept locked and there is no access to the tower except for the ringers of the six bells. The helpful verger who trusted me with the key told me there had been a bell practice the night before.

Even from the ground the view in every direction is a sensation. To the south the Mendips and beyond them the Quantock Hills (but not on my day). West and north west the Severn estuary and beyond it the Welsh Hills. The modern Severn Bridge and Brunel's Memorial designed by himself for Charing Cross—the famous Clifton Suspension Bridge over the Avon Gorge.

Whatever may be thought of modern Bristol it looks very impressive from this point. And practically every point of vantage in Bristol can look up to the tower of Dundry.

Lavenham Church, Suffolk

You can see it for miles round. It stands at the higher end of the antique village of Lavenham, once a prosperous market town devoted principally to the cloth trade. Cloth and king-making are the two sources of wealth that paid for the building of Lavenham.

In 1485 John de Vere, 13th Earl of Oxford, having helped to establish Henry Tudor on the throne of England, wished to give thanks to God with a fine church on one of his many manors (which included Hedingham in Essex with its great Norman keep). Material help came from the 'rich clothier' Thomas Spryng II, and his son, another Thomas, and this great perpendicular edifice was erected all of a piece between 1485 and 1525, leaving only the Decorated chancel and its small, slender tower topped by a crocketed finial from the earlier church.

The West tower is Suffolk's highest at 141 feet, and yet it is unfinished. Look at those square projections at each corner of the sub-parapet at the top. They are plinths on which turrets or pinnacles should rest and within that square, flat top at least a conical roof should rise, if not a spire.

Did the money run out? It is more likely that here, as elsewhere, the onset of the Reformation halted further adornment. Southwold and many lesser East Anglian towers of the period share this flat-topped characteristic. Perhaps at Lavenham the hatless severity adds to the tower's dignity.

The de Vere connection is evident in the South porch and frequently within by the carved heraldic devices: the molet, or five-pointed star, and the boar.

This interests me because I am descended from those earls of Oxford. The last of their line, an heiress, married the 1st Duke of St Albans, son of Charles II and Nell Gwynn. So I have the Drury Lane chorus line as well as the stars in my blood.

The younger Thomas Spryng is remembered by the delicately carved oak parclose at the north-east end of the nave, though the flat tombstone within is not his. There are also modern Spryng tablets within the parclose, in memory (1933) of Sir Francis Spring, K.C.I.E. 10th in descent from Thomas, and of Merelina Spring-Stanley, 1938.

The proportions of the church are worthy of the fine advertisement provided by the tower, and there are occasional concerts of very high quality.

Layer Marney Tower, Essex

This, believe it or not, was built as a gatehouse, between 1520 and 1523.

It was also, at 80 feet in height, reputed to be one of the tallest load-bearing brick buildings until, a few years ago, the residential tower blocks of Essex University nearby were run up, to achieve a new record and to the later dismay of the moral guardians of the University.

Marneys had been at Layer Marney for centuries when the first Lord Marney, Captain of the Bodyguard to Henry VII and Henry VIII, erected this conceit, planned as the entrance to the courtyard of a massive dwelling. This was never built. Lord Marney died in 1523 and his son the second Lord Marney in 1525, when the place passed to the Tuke family, who held it for only half a century. Later Tukes joined the Quaker persuasion. Since then it has had many owners.

Apart from great height Layer Marney has another feature of distinction. The mullions of the windows, and the friezes, and the scallops and dolphins and pineapples of the parapets, are of terracotta. This was a startling innovation at the time, and of direct Italian Renaissance influence, probably due to the presence at Court of the Italian architect Girolamo da Trevizi. Continuing in this style after Henry VIII got cross with Rome might have been unwise. But there it was, and there it still is. As the present owner explains, terracotta weathers better than carved stone because, like the brickwork, it has been fired.

The pictures you see are of the southern towers; those facing north are also impressive but more severe. Side wings, contemporary but for a well-considered Edwardian range, have more terracotta work. Even this example of vertical emphasis was designed as part of a horizontal whole.

Originally you drove through the archways which now frame the garden door to the south and the front door to the north, now with stone flagged hall between. A scraping of the northern archway shows evidence of careless driving long ago.

When you visit, do not hurry away; visit also the brick-built church in the grounds, which has some terracotta work in the window dressings. Within, the canopies and friezes of the Marney monuments are also in terracotta.

Evesham Bell Tower, Worcestershire

In company with several hundred refugees from Hitler's Europe, some of whom have since become notable in Britain, I toiled at Evesham for more than two wartime years in the BBC Monitoring Service. Despite its closeness to tea shops and favourite pubs I paid scant attention to Evesham's wonderful Bell Tower until it was forcefully drawn to my attention by Canon Allsebrook, a relation of one of my workmates.

First conceived by Abbot Lichfield, the last Abbot of Evesham, it now serves as the call to worship in the two neighbouring parish churches of All Saints' and St. Laurence. For such an ornate structure to be built so late as 1529 to 1539 is a tribute to the calmness of the builders in the time of the ugly face of the Reformation. Evesham Abbey had been dissolved before its completion.

Some purists consider the panelling, so evenly distributed over the whole of the north and south faces, including the buttresses, to be excessive and monotonous. The top stage is panelled on all four sides and is even continued in the perforated design of the parapet. To me the whole structure is unusually elevating. There is a ring of 12 bells, recast in 1951. There is also a carillon.

Originally a roadway passed below the campanile archway. The handsome ogee arches are at every level; the same feature can also be seen at Chipping Campden, high in the Cotswolds nearby and a landmark for miles. But at Campden they are only at the topmost level, piercing the parapet with finials.

Evesham tower is hardly noticed in the bustle of the town, not greatly above the level of the River Avon passing through the Vale of Evesham only a little over 70 feet above sea level.

To the south looms the bulk of Bredon Hill, to the north the Lench Hills with their scattering of improbably named villages and hamlets—Church Lench, Rous Lench, Sheriffs Lench, Ab Lench, Atch Lench (where I lived) and, more on a level with the Avon, Lenchwick.

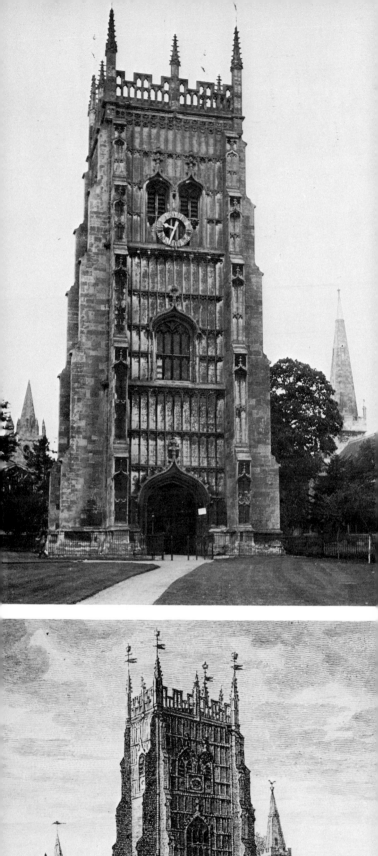

Freston Tower, Suffolk

Standing at the summit of a steep parkscape where cattle graze, above the south bank of the Orwell estuary downstream from Ipswich port, Freston Tower is probably the oldest folly of them all. But what is a folly? White's Suffolk Guide of 1844 gives a clue: 'This quadrangular brick building, six stories high, containing as many rooms, one above another, but only about 10 feet by 12, with a polygonal turret at each angle, terminating in pinnacles; and a winding turret staircase projecting from the western side, and terminating in an octagonal lantern . . . There is but one fire place, which is on the ground floor . . . and no chimney; hence it is probable that this building was rather an occasional pleasure retreat, or watch tower, than a place of permanent habitation'.

Just so. The property of Freston Park was acquired in 1553 from the Latimer family by Thos. Gooding, an Ipswich merchant, and it is supposed that he used it, even if he did not build it himself, to observe the shipping passing between Ipswich and the sea. His ships? Or ships carrying his goods?

Early in June 1944, craft engaged in the D-Day Normandy landings passed down this navigable estuary, and residents at the farm-house near by had to have special passes to get to and fro.

The brickwork is undoubtedly Tudor, but the exact date of the building is unknown. It is still privately owned, and is converted into a modernised residence. Approached by a rough track, or a tangle of footpaths from the southern side, the best view, showing the fenestration of each of the six floors, is from the north-west, sloping steeply away towards Ipswich. There is no public access.

Ardvreck, Sutherland

After Charles I's execution in 1649 James Graham, Marquis of Montrose, plotted and planned his return from exile to continue the royal cause in Scotland. He landed in Orkney early in 1650 with a few hundred Scandinavians, recruited as many more Orcadians and crossed to the mainland. Government forces engaged him at Carbisdale, at the head of the Dornoch Firth, and he was hopelessly defeated, fled to the Sutherland hills with two companions, was lost, exhausted after two days wandering, and came upon a shieling where he asked the farmer for milk. He was given whisky instead and, much refreshed, asked to be directed to Reay, to the north, where he might escape to Orkney. As he drank, his countryman's cloak, an inefficient disguise, fell open to reveal some martial decoration and he was recognised. He was guided and directed instead to Ardvreck Castle, by Loch Assynt.

Ardvreck was built around 1590 by the MacLeods of Assynt, that weird country of strange mountains with strange names: Quinag, Canisp, Suilven and Stac Pollaidh, the last two tower-like themselves from certain prospects. Built on a spit of land jutting into Loch Assynt from a natural causeway, the ruin of Ardvreck is still a lonely and forbidding place.

Some historians have accepted the view that young Neil MacLeod of Assynt gave Montrose away for the price on his head. The MacLeods have a different story. Young Assynt, a Covenanter, was miles away helping the Earl of Sutherland in the siege of the Sinclair castle of Dunbeath on the Caithness cliffs and now the comfortable home of a delightful American family. When Montrose arrived Neil's wife had him clapped in the Ardvreck dungeon and sent messengers to her husband and to the local Government H.Q.

On 4 May Montrose was escorted by General Holbourn to Edinburgh; on 21 May 1650, he was executed at the Mercat Cross and his head stuck on a pole. Six years earlier my direct ancestor Sir John Gordon of Haddo seems to have been the first to suffer the same fate for the same cause in the same place.

On 28 June the Scottish Parliament agreed Assynt's reward of £20,000 Scots and 400 bolls of meal. Whether he got either is disputed. After the Restoration of 1660 he was twice tried, unsuccessfully, for betraying Montrose. These and other physical and legal harryings by the Seaforth MacKenzies, his principal enemies, exhausted this unimportant chieftain, and he died in poverty in Edinburgh in 1696.

Ardvreck's solitary ruins stand as a worn monument to tragedies. I cannot adjudicate between historians and the vigorous case of the Clan MacLeod. Montrose was too ardent in his attempt; Assynt was in a trap either way. Ardvreck, now, is a sorry wreck. Contrary to many appearances, men are more abiding, of greater matter, than stone and mortar.

The Tron Kirk, Edinburgh

The Tolbooth stands high along the Royal Mile in Edinburgh, close to the Castle precincts. Near the dreadful place stands the prominent spire of the nineteenth-century Highland Kirk. Lower down is St. Giles' Cathedral, the principal kirk for centuries of the Church of Scotland. A little below that is the Trongate. A tron is a market weighing machine. On an island site at this spot the foundation stone of the Tron Kirk was laid in 1637, the date on the entablature of the entrance is 1641, from which we may safely date its original tower.

It was rebuilt in its present form after the Great Fire of Edinburgh in 1824 and, blackened and eaten by the smoke of Auld Reekie, was renovated in 1977. The City of Edinburgh spent much money on this work. The kirk is now disused, but it is planned that when money can be spent it will be reopened for secular use; lectures, exhibitions and the like. It will be worthwhile to get in the queue for that inauguration.

It was within sight of the Tron Kirk that the execution of Montrose took place at the Mercat, or Market, Cross. He had a horrible journey from Ardvreck to this place, being first of all received with courteous hospitality, but later at each stopping place he was more and more humiliated. Whether or not this was a deliberate degradation, he met his end with noble bearing and a fine speech. After 1660 his blackened and rotting head was replaced by that of Argyll, the undoubted leader of the Presbyterian adherents of the Protector.

Top: the renovated Tron Kirk
Bottom: before the Fire of 1824

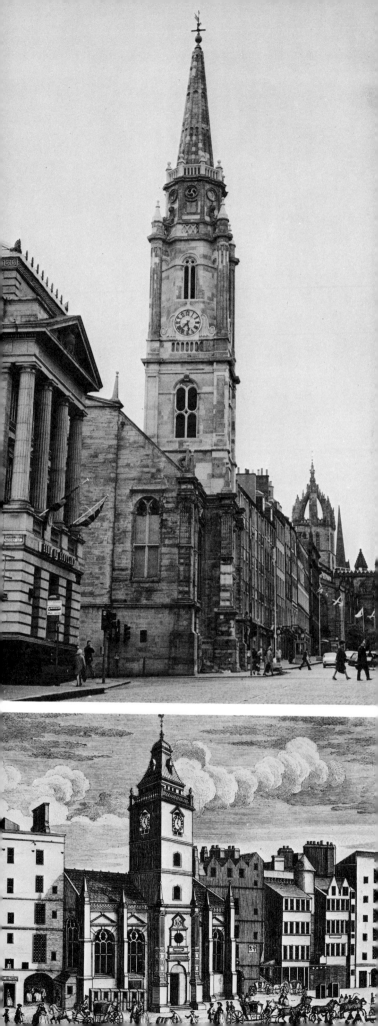

Craigievar Castle, Aberdeenshire

Completed in 1626, Craigievar Castle in Aberdeenshire is the latest, and the finest by far, of the castle houses of the Scottish Renaissance. You might suppose that this was the ingenious creation of an aristocrat. So, at the beginning, it was to have been, but the impoverished Mortimer family had to leave it to be completed by William Forbes—'Willie the merchant' or 'Danzig Willie' he was called—who in 1610 took over the property and the partly built castle, which was probably carried out by a remarkable Aberdeen mastermason, John Bell.

Willie the merchant was no upstart. A direct ancestor had been armour bearer to King James III, and he was a younger son of Forbes of Corse. Younger sons, of course, often had to make their own way, usually serving under arms or in the Church. He chose commerce, and his success was rewarded by the creation of this matchless dwelling. He lived only one year to enjoy it, dying in 1627.

Just look at those thick walls of granite, pink-harled, smooth and undecorated until you reach the corbel-belt cornice and the corbelling below the uprising turrets and cupolas and crow-stepped gables pointing to the sky. The cupola is 74 feet high.

Nobody could doubt that you are, here, deep in the fringe of that country where the Scottish lowland families and the Gaelic highlanders touched and raided each other for cattle and other victuals. A fortified house was customary at that time in such a place. Nevertheless, it is a dwelling of unusual comfort and convenience compared with most of the habitations of seventeenth-century Scotland, and since it has been so little messed about within, you can tell that it was a place of elegant appointment from the beginning. The great hall, especially, though a Gothic vault in conception, has much Renaissance plaster and stucco work.

There are stories of vile feuding and enmity between the Forbes families who were mostly Covenanters, and my tribe the Gordons, mostly Royalists. One Gordon may have been thrown out of a high window, probably caught in a lady's room where he had no business. But all that anger is in the past.

In February 1934 Lord Sempill, the Forbes owner of Craigievar, died. My grandfather, in the winter weather, insisted on attending the funeral of his younger contemporary and old friend. It was my grandfather's last outing. A week later he, too, died. My grandfather's house, which he built in 1905 against his retirement, is no more. Craigievar lives on. For ever, I guess.

St. Bride's Church, Fleet Street, London

The conflict of 1939–45 put an end to any prospect of the Third Reich lasting a thousand years. Through the bombing of London, the war added nearly a thousand years to the history of this church, which is the journalists' shrine, and pride.

On 29 December 1940 the body of the church of St. Bride's was reduced to a shellful of rubble; Wren's steeple was harmed but unbowed. For 17 years the church operated on a hutted basis. Then, under the supervision of the architect Godfrey Allen assisted by John R. Stammers, a new church in the spirit of Wren but not exactly copying his original, was re-dedicated on 19 December 1957.

Meanwhile, when the rubble had been cleared away, archaeologists were brought in to probe and sift the foundations. A Roman pavement was discovered, and a Roman building. Was it perhaps some early Christian shrine without the City Wall? A sixth-century church of stone was found, dedicated to St. Bridget or Brigit, born in 453 in Kildare. She must have known the earliest Irish Round Towers. So the Celtic and the Roman Churches strangely met on this spot.

The Great Fire of London in 1666 did far more damage than Hitler's bombs, and on the burnt-out site Sir Christopher completed in 1675 this church and his tallest steeple, originally 234 feet from pavement to top. Subtract eight feet for damage by lightning in 1702 and you can calculate today's height.

Many people dismissively refer to the steeple as the wedding cake—too obvious a pun—without appreciating the genius by which Wren applied classical motifs to Gothic form.

When I was a young journalist before the war I shared a backroom office in a rundown building farther west along Fleet Street. When inspiration failed I could lean too far out of the window and gaze upon this heavenly steeple. For further refreshment it was easy, and still is, to cross Fleet Street and stand by Poppin's Court, just below the Express Building, to stare at the pencil-slim black steeple of St. Martin's-within-Ludgate halfway up Ludgate Hill, cunningly placed by Wren to be seen in silhouette, appearing from that point to be pricking the great dome of St Paul's.

St. Stephen's Walbrook is only a little farther away, behind the Mansion House, now with the Samaritan Centre presided over by the Very Rev. Chad Varah. Its dome possibly was Wren's model for St. Paul's. Its tower, with lantern and slim central pinnacle, looks doll-like compared with surrounding monsters, yet the total height is 135 feet.

Yet another pleasure of my youth was to listen to a lunch-time organ recital and then eat sandwiches from Jolly's (no more) in the churchyard of St. Michael's, Cornhill, which Hawksmoor completed from Wren's start.

The London Monument

The London Monument commemorates the Great Fire of London in 1666, and coincidentally celebrates the release of London from the centuries' old recurrence of the Plague. It was designed by Sir Christopher Wren and completed in 1677. It was placed in the line of approach from the City side to Old London Bridge, and when this was rebuilt westward of the old structure the Monument lost its fine position, and is now to be found rising, in Monument Place, from the obscurity of Fish Street Hill.

An inscription at the base, among other wordage in Latin on three panels of the great square plinth, records that the fire broke out 'at a distance eastward from this place of 202 feet which is the height of this column'. The fourth face of the plinth shows an heroic sculptured relief by Cibber. Pudding Lane, where the fire began, still exists as a name, and the Monument survived the bombs of 1940–45. It is now cleaned, repaired and burnished.

It is a fluted Doric column in Portland stone, rising from a pedestal 40 feet high. The fluted shaft is 120 feet high and 15 feet in diameter. On the abacus is a balcony surrounding a moulded cylinder which supports a flaming urn of gilt bronze, to remind you of the Fire.

To reach the balcony a stone spiral stairway of 311 steps must be trod. The walls are covered with the grafitti of countless visitors. One John Quigley seems to have signed in at least six places. Perhaps he needed several rests. I did, and was grateful for the periodic official plates saying how many steps had been climbed. The view is, as usual in London now from these ancient eminences, a poor reward.

The balcony is encased in an iron cage, to prevent the suicides of long ago. It was put there in 1842. The *Daily Journal* of 16 September 1732 records a sailor's adventure :
'Yesterday, about 5 o'clock in the evening, notwithstanding the wind was so high, a sailor flew from the top of the Monument to the Upper Three Tuns Tavern in Gracechurch Street, which he did in less than half a minute; there was a numerous crowd of spectators to see him. He came down within 20 feet of the place where the rope was fixed, and then flung himself off; and offered, if the gentlemen would make him a handsome collection, he would go up and fly down again'.

The only way to damage yourself now is to drop down the spiral well of the stair. Poking a head over the iron baluster is enough to show the accuracy of trajectory needed for such a drop. On the way down you watch your tread, not the grafitti. The climb and descent are so impressive that the many visitors progressing in both directions are smiling and polite, grateful perhaps for a shared intent to survive the journeys.

The Castletown Folly, Co. Kildare

Two centuries before John Maynard Keynes advocated programmes of public works to relieve unemployment and to create inconspicuous consumption; one century before Samuel Smiles's *Self Help, with Illustrations of Conduct and Character*, Mrs Conolly in Ireland got the right idea.

The winter of 1739–40 in Ireland had been disastrously severe. People were cold and starving. Mrs Conolly, widow of a Mr Speaker of the Irish Parliament, looked out from Castletown House at Celbridge in County Kildare and saw possibilities. In her day it would have been quite wrong just to give money to the cold and hungry, so that they could clothe and feed themselves. Work must be found for the men. So she set about building.

The chief consequence of her practical imagination can claim to be the outstanding eyecatcher-cum-obelisk in our islands. It stands on high ground about two miles from Mr Speaker Conolly's Castletown House, built in 1720 by Allessandro Galilei and Sir Edward Pearce. Pearce's assistant Richard Castle is thought to have designed the folly; it has been diligently kept good by the Irish Georgian Society.

In grey stone mottled by lichens it is an improbable structure which achieves a daring unity. From ground level rise five round arches, the large central one set forward, flanked by recessed arches of less importance, and with small outliers also set boldly forward, either crowned with a cupola. On top of the recessed arches are two more arches, their flat cornices having little obelisks, on which eagles perch, rising from them.

Above the central arch is a square chamber with a pediment from which there soars the tapering obelisk to a height of 140 feet. It is like a pyramid of circus acrobats in stone, and very pretty too. Mrs Conolly's sister must have thought this folly foolish, and she was wrong.

She wrote to a friend: 'My sister is building an Obleix to answer a Vistoe from the Bake of Castletown. It will cost her 3 or 4 hundred pounds at least, and I believe more. I don't know how she can dow so much and live as she duse'.

Mrs. Conolly lived to 'dow' a good deal more. There was famine still, so the lean years must prepare for the fat ones. She built the Wonderful Barn. It has the appearance of a fat-bottomed bottle with an outside stone staircase spiralling up to its crown. It looks mad but is not. The idea was to store grain in the good years in a series of domed chambers within. It is still in use.

Mrs Conolly was not the only Irish folly builder whose object was famine relief, but I would have loved her best. She must have been quite different from the pitiless and relentless soul snatchers of the Victorian age and after.

The Folly

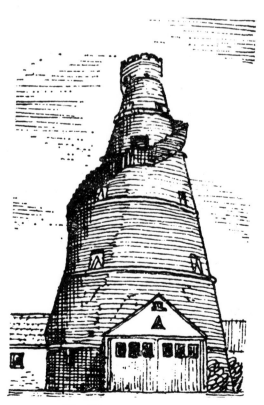

The Wonderful Barn

The Dunmore Pineapple, Stirling

The taxi driver was invited to take us from Stirling to see the Pineapple in Dunmore Park a few miles away. Yes, he knew Dunmore village, but a pineapple? In stone? He turned left into a newish village housing estate, in the centre of which is a park, a roughly triangular piece of grass with some swings and other playground delights.

A handy council gardener redirected us, and there was the familiar signboard of the National Trust for Scotland in blue: TO THE PINEAPPLE. A bumpy drive leads to a hardcore car park and the entrance to a large walled garden. The south-facing brick wall is very high, and is cavity built, to help in the heating of the glasshouses which it once supported.

Here, in the eighteenth century, pineapples were successfully grown and, to celebrate this triumph, this most wise of follies was built in 1761, by an architect now unknown. It is 45 feet high from garden level, supported by a simple pediment over a Venetian arch. Above is an octagonal chamber, perhaps a little banquet room, with eight ogee windows with curved panes. The stone carving of this huge fruit is somewhat formalised but convincing and elaborately certain of itself.

The small room inside is of quite plain dressed stone with a domed ceiling. Scattered about were a few ordinary deckchairs, and that seemed quite in keeping with the fantasy outside. So did the sprouting willow herb growing from one of the cone-like knobs, such a nuisance to remove when preparing the best pudding— slices of pineapple marinated in equal amounts of castor sugar and kirsch.

That old familiar Christopher Colombus discovered the pineapple in 1493. This one was bought and presented to the National Trust for Scotland by the Earl and Countess of Perth. A warm and, I daresay, rather expensive gesture. The taxi driver was delighted by his discovery; he would bring the family along to see it at the first chance.

Pineapples were a status symbol long before Arnold Bennett insisted that there should always be one at his table. Was not Charles II painted receiving one? And they are a familiar motif carved on gateposts and along walls, on staircases, on wallpaper, along friezes, anywhere. Why pineapple? The Spaniards called it Pinaslas-India, corrupted into English as pineapple and now universally known as *Ananas comosus*. 'Comosus' means furnished with a tuft.

Kew Pagoda, London

The Chinese taste was slow to catch on in England. In architecture there were modest glimmerings of it in the seventeenth century, but nothing much. Early in the eighteenth century it was given a push by an able landscape and architectural publicist with the odd name of Batty Langley; by the 1750s everybody was at it.

In 1757 William Chambers published a treatise on Chinese buildings and other useful artefacts. At that time Chambers also got the post of architectural tutor to the Prince of Wales, who became George III in 1760. Almost at once the King made William Chambers—a knighthood came later—and Robert Adam Joint Architects of His Majesty's Works.

Chambers designed Kew Pagoda in 1761 and up it went in what is now the Royal Botanic Gardens. It must have looked less solemn then. Dragons projecting from each of the ten roofs were covered in a film of multi-coloured glass which gave a dazzling reflection, and each roof stage with iron sheeting varnished in many hues. The dragons are now gone and the roofs are slate. The whingding on top was gilded.

The basic structure is of stock brick, the tapering is one foot at each level and the total height 163 feet. Inside, a central wooden tower staircase is solid and secure, likewise the floorboards at every level. Nevertheless there is no public access. From the top it is easy to see across the Thames to Syon House, where Adam was working for the Duke of Northumberland at about the time the Pagoda was completed.

When I was very young and first lived in London I often went to Kew. On one occasion I fell in with a gaunt white-haired man, most knowledgeable about plants and a help to my education. Would I come home to tea? Well, yes certainly. (There was nothing else to do.) We travelled for ages by District Line to East London, and while his wife was making tea he took me into a tiny garden and brought from the neat shed a model of the Pagoda, made of card and matchsticks, entirely covered with multi-coloured foil. It may not have been exact but it was a good deal more cheerful than the original as it then was.

On a dismal day I was escorted to this very stolid, English-looking piece of Chinoiserie by a lady who kindly deserted her warm office at Kew to take me up. It was pleasant to see all the woodwork newly painted a bright vermilion or cinnabar red. Horizontal surfaces and the roof ribs were in darkest blue. A good combination.

In my youth it cost a penny to enter Kew. It still does. One new penny, of course. To get there by District Line from Liverpool Street now costs nearly a hundred times as much.

Top: the Pagoda today
Bottom: Chambers's design for the Pagoda

Brizlee Folly,
Alnwick, Northumberland

A chance photograph, the lens uptilted, showed that perhaps Robert Adam had designed a tower which was a fussy muddle. Accepting that Mr Adam's elegant insides are usually more satisfactory than his outsides, on which his fastidious decorations often are too dainty for the façades, a determination set in to find out whether Robert Adams had in fact done something ugly. I was glad to be quite wrong.

Hulne Park, on the opposite side of the little town of Alnwick from the Duke of Northumberland's great castle, forms the pleasure grounds of this demesne. On a tree-clad hill at its centre this 80-foot tower rises just above the tree line. Somewhat in need of repair, but perfectly sound, it cleverly combines classical form and 'Gothick' detail.

A spiral stone stair leads to the viewing gallery, from which on a clear day it is claimed that you can see seven castles—Alnwick itself, Bamburgh, Callaly, Chillingham, Dunstanburgh, Lindisfarne and Warkworth. Alas! for me; on the day of my visit there was a thick mist and the *Rhododendron ponticum* which has spread and seeded everywhere dripped dismal moisture.

Robert Adam did much work at Alnwick for the 1st Duke, bullied into it by the Duchess, so the Percy family say. The design for Brizlee is dated 1778. Perhaps he needed only a little bullying, since he had years ago had the commission virtually to refashion Syon House, on the Middlesex bank of the Thames opposite the King's little palace at Kew, and Kew Gardens with Chambers's Pagoda. Chambers, a scholar of the Renaissance full of *gravitas*, was scornful of the shallow Adam inventions. I wonder what he thought of the lion statant—the Percy crest—on the screen at Syon House. Wonder, too, at what Adam thought of the far from scholarly Kew Pagoda. The lion now on the roof of Syon House was put there in 1874, brought from Northumberland House on the Strand when that palace of the Percys was pulled down.

Everybody should see the Brizlee Folly. Access is on foot only, but Hulne Park is always open, and can lead you to this exquisitely detailed object. It is so slender there is no space for even the smallest banquet room; not even a deckchair as in the Dunmore Pineapple.

Glenfinnan Monument, Fort William, Highland

The glory of the monument is not the view from it but the view of it in its setting. It is impossible to do better than to quote the description by Miss Wendy Wood, a pioneer Scottish Nationalist, in her *Moidart and Morar* : 'The monument that was raised to the men who fought for Prince Charles Edward Stuart stands upon a green sward in an amphitheatre of lordly hills . . . The waters of Loch Shiel terminate at the foot of the column like a silver indicator, 18 miles in length . . . from its farthest end the blazoned banners of sunsets salute the memory of the Standard of the Stuarts . . . Nothing can affect the grandeur of the place'.

The Rising of the '45 nearly did not take place. The bonny Prince landed from a French frigate with seven loyal supporters and few supplies. Much equipment had been turned back when the escorting French warship was engaged and damaged by an English man-o'-war, which also suffered. Assembled MacDonalds and others counselled calling the whole thing off. To what good could they proceed? No army had arrived with the Prince, and only a few guns ripped off the frigate.

A combination of obstinacy and youthful charm on the one hand, a magisterial appeal to loyalty affecting men with little to lose on the other, tipped the scales in favour of 'that arduous and unfortunate enterprise', part of the wording on the monument. Unlike the Bourbons, the Stuarts seem to have forgotten a lot, and learned too little.

The quick history that followed moves far away from Glenfinnan, but in little over a year Charles Edward embarked from that same sea loch at which he had arrived, after being a fugitive in sight of Glenfinnan, in another French frigate inaptly named *L'Heureux*.

The whole story is a confusion. Names, proper and improper, too, can be confusing. The seven men of Moidart were men all right, and there is the silver indicator of Loch Shiel. Far to the north, in Wester Ross, are the Five Sisters of Kintail, not noble women, but prickly peaks bounding the north face of Glen Shiel. A harsh place where, in 1719, below the stony skirts of those hills, another Jacobite attempt to win back the Crown, that time aided by a Spanish ship which was quickly blown to smithereens, was defeated only days after the landing at the sea loch of Duich.

Here, jutting into the sea, is the Castle of Eilean Donan, which was also reduced. Now it has been sumptuously restored at great cost. The Five Sisters eternally look down on it; the men of Morar and their more humble supporters are remembered at Glenfinnan.

The monument was built in 1815; the 18-foot Highlander atop was added later. It is unsatisfactory; he looks like a huge Liberace dressed in a kilt.

Quex Park, Birchington-on-Sea, Kent

Birchington, on the whole, is a bore. It lacks the distinction given to its neighbour Westgate-on-Sea, with its white painted wooden balconies, of being celebrated by Sir John Betjeman, and there is none of the Georgian remains and the Cockney fun of Margate. Who, now, remembers Margate Sands Railway Station?

Birchington has the first purpose-built bungalows in England, which are of interest to architectural specialists. Dante Gabriel Rossetti died in one of them in 1882, and is remembered.

Birchington also has the Waterloo or Bell Tower in Quex Park, little more than a mile from the sea. The tower itself is a belfry and is square, of red brick with stone dressings. It is hemmed in by four octagonal turrets with cast-iron battlements. From these turrets spring the cast-iron legs of a miniature Eiffel Tower, the lattice work precise and white painted, topped by a gilded ball and weathervane.

During childhood holidays at Westgate it was possible once or twice to slope off alone on a bicycle to look at this pretty object. In my ignorance I thought it copied from the Eiffel Tower in Paris. I may even have toasted it in Eiffel Tower lemonade. I wonder if that is still made?

Nothing could be further from the truth than my childhood guess. It was built by the rich John Powell-Powell Esq, and opened to the public on 4 August 1819. It is worth close inspection and needs it because of the trees round the tower, which houses a peal of twelve bells. It is a favourite meeting place of bell ringers, organised by All Saints Church, Birchington. It is not open to the public but can be seen from afar, and also in a close view from the lane nearby.

The authors of the Eiffel Tower probably knew little of Quex, and Messrs Read, Maxwell and Tuke, responsible for the Blackpool Tower, even less. The Eiffel dates from 1889, and is 984 feet high. England's answer was completed in 1894 at a mere 518 feet. It must be 25 years since I first went up Blackpool Tower in its creaking and wobbly lift. On the viewing platform a west wind from the Irish Sea was uncomfortably strong, but it was worth it for the view across the flat Fylde farmland to the Forest of Bowland and the Lancashire Hills. The Isle of Man was invisible. Blackpool was spread out below and it was too early for the illuminations.

The autumn spectacle of the illuminations, with the comic tableaux of moving trams, must have been devised as a means of attracting visitors out of season, and of consuming electricity at night, when industrial demand is not so heavy.

Top left: the Waterloo Tower in multiple exposure
Top right: the Waterloo Tower
Bottom: Blackpool Tower

Lansdown Tower, Bath

After William Beckford had sold the immense Gothic folly of Fonthill Abbey, one house in Bath—for a while two houses—was not enough for him. He bought a mile-long strip of land behind his new home in Lansdown Crescent, leading to the summit—nearly 800 feet—of Lansdown Hill.

There, in 1825, he set about building Lansdown Tower. The dying contractor of Wyatt's central octagon and dotty tower at Fonthill had confessed that he had cheated and skimped the foundations.

After the building of this new tower had begun the old one, expression of a fortune in sugar and an imagination superheated, fell. The fatuous Mr. Cube would have laughed probably, and Beckford did not care. He was busy on the new project. Always in a hurry with his building, he chose as his architect an unknown young man, H. E. Goodridge, more pliant to his ideas than any fashionable London master. The combination of the two worked; the building survives and so did their friendship to the end of Beckford's life.

According to Goodridge's son it was up to the level of the great square cornice within a month. Then a roof? No, it was not high enough. A 'Belvidere', please, something like this. Beckford was active in design and Goodridge obeyed. More yet had to be added, a lantern. Take the Lysicrates Monument in Athens as a model, and do something different, original. At 154 feet the restless, querulous man who was at his iciest calm when others were excited, was satisfied.

During the rush to build, the workmen suddenly downed tools, so the story goes. According to a letter from a Bath gossip to John Constable, they had got a whiff of a homosexual scandal of Beckford's far-distant youth, and refused to work for him. More likely the bustle and hurry and long hours and constant changes of plan, without benefit of overtime and danger money, were the real cause. Goodridge somehow placated the builders and the work went on. It was completed in 1827.

Here was the perfect retreat for a reclusive rich man, away from the smoky, now seedy city, no longer fashionable. There are great views in almost every direction, but that was only part of the point. A garden contrived to look wild was laid out, and within the two square blocks at the foot of the Tower were the crimson drawing room, the scarlet drawing room, the Etruscan library and much else rich and rare. Everything was removed or sold after Beckford's death and now, after periods of neglect and inadequate repair, all is well again. There are two residences formed from Beckford's apartments, and a museum created, first under the ownership of Dr and Mrs L. T. Hilliard and now under the Beckford Tower Trust which they set up in 1977. There is public access from April to October at weekends, except to the topmost cupola.

Net Towers, Hastings, Sussex

Clustered together like New York skyscrapers, these tall huts are aesthetically pleasing, as well as quaint. Their close grouping is the point, and has attracted artists over a long period. There is a practical reason for their shape, and the huddle of them. Early in the seventeenth century Hastings Corporation let out small plots on the stony beach to fishermen, who at the time were suffering from poverty. These men built tall to use well the small space they could hire, just enough for a 'deeze' or shop, with a working space in front.

It is believed that they are modelled on Scandinavian huts, because of some characteristics of their construction. Weather-boarded and tarred, they are long lasting —nobody knows the age of the present towers—and some of the original leases have survived.

To me they have two associations. The first is of eating a dish of sprats with friends living in Old Hastings, deep fried and succulent. The other is of two great uncles, dead long before I was born.

The 6th Earl of Aberdeen, George, and his brother James, as very young men, set out in April 1865 from this beach at night in a rowing skiff, determined to cross to Boulogne and back. They got into trouble with the French douanes and nearly lost their lives in bad weather when they were sent packing for the return journey. They had not long to wait. James was killed at Cambridge in 1868 through carelessness with his rifle.

George cut loose from these shores for ever in 1866 and spent four years sailing with the United States Merchant Marine. Six days out from Boston in 1870 he was swept overboard in a storm whilst serving as first mate in a three-masted schooner bound for Australia. Did he remember Hastings, the starting point of his dangerous seafaring life?

Windmills

The great concentration of surviving windmills is in the eastern half of England, though there is a sprinkling of them in the west and in Wales. They are of three types : the post mill on a brick or stone base and clad in weatherboarding; the tower mill built of brick or stone; and the smock mill, also weatherboarded, and often octagonal. All three types may have a gallery running round their midriff like a sash, and some are galleried just below the cap.

The survivors are mostly not very old, nineteenth century for the most part and often built on the site of earlier mills. In recent years there has been a commendable amount of restoration work done on some of the more historically valuable, some are still working and a few have been converted into dwellings.

They are mostly not of great height, but with their sails rising above their caps, and being located in prominent positions, they look higher than they are.

There is little doubt that windmills were originally introduced to England from the continent, and no doubt at all that in the eighteenth and nineteenth centuries English ironfounding and engineering skills were exported to northwest Europe to improve and modernise their working parts.

The term windmill includes those structures devoted not to the milling of corn, but to drainage and irrigation. An example of one of these is the well known Berney Arms Mill at Reedham near Great Yarmouth in Norfolk. This is a drainage mill built of brick and over 70 feet high. It is in the care of the Ancient Monuments Board and can be reached by rail or water, but not by motor car.

The Union Mill, Cranbrook, Kent
This smock mill dominates the little town of Cranbrook and is the largest, though not the tallest, mill in England. It is 70 feet high, just short of the tower mill at Sutton in Norfolk, which reaches almost 80 feet. It was built in 1814 and the frame is original. The four sweeps, as sails are called in Kent, were taken from the mill at Sarre on the edge of Thanet in 1922. Work was done on them after the war by the owner, the late John Russell, millwright as well as miller, and in 1958 the Society for the Protection of Ancient Buildings, which has had a lively Windmill Section for many years, carried out restoration work with help from the Kent County Council.

Despite its great girth it has fine proportions with its well-placed gallery, and deserves its eminence as an elegant working monument which has put its protective skirt over the ingeniously contrived machinery. When I went to see it work was going on, machinery was whirring, but the sweeps were still.

The smock mill at Cranbrook

Saxtead Green, near Framlingham, Suffolk

Rising above a brick roundhouse, this weatherboarded post mill which stands back from the broad green at Saxtead is probably the finest and certainly the most carefully preserved of its kind. It is now an ancient monument. There are medieval references to a mill on this site, but the earliest reference to the present mill is in 1796. The miller's house beside it was built in 1810.

In Suffolk the casing of a post mill is called the 'buck' and here, as elsewhere, all is painted white except for the black base of the roundhouse. The mill has been lifted three times in its history to raise the level of the roundhouse, the third time to accommodate a supplementary steam engine.

Mr Rex Wailes, a leading authority on mills who saw it working when it belonged to the Aldred family, regards it as one of the finest post mills in the world, and has no quarrel with the preservative work carried out for the Ancient Monuments Board. Visit if possible on a quiet day. The intricacies of machinery and ladders are too intimate to be enjoyed amongst a horde.

Farther to the west, near Bury St Edmunds, Pakenham tower mill is also listed as an ancient monument and continues to be worked by the millers who own it, J. Bryant and Sons. A water mill in the same small village now belongs to the Suffolk Preservation Society, who have undertaken to restore it and put its original machinery back into working order.

Top: the tower mill at Pakenham
Bottom: the post mill at Saxtead Green

Big Ben and The Towers of Westminster

It was the Day of Prorogation, when one session of Parliament was ended a week before the Queen opened the new session. I was late for the ceremony. I was doing a little research for this very page high up in the Victoria Tower, in the Parliamentary Record Office, and when you are looking through old papers and pictures it is easy to let time go by.

It was impossible for me to get to my seat in the House of Lords Chamber, for standing behind the Bar were the Commons assembled, blocking effective entry. Whilst the Lord Chancellor, bewigged and hatted, was reciting the achievements of the session, I stood, patiently attending amongst a crowd of Commoners, behind Mr Callaghan and Mrs Thatcher. Then the Clerk of the Parliaments read out the Sovereign's message proroguing Parliament and telling us when to come back. This was in October 1978.

Next morning, sharp at 11.30 by arrangement, I joined a very small party of Mr Michael Foot's constituents to be guided up the Clock Tower. It would be silly to try to describe the outside of this most famous of all towers, and I quote briefly about its inside from an excellent illustrated volume of 1865 :

'The interior arrangement of the Tower comprises a stone staircase at its west angle, from the ground to the level of the floor of the bell lantern; a shaft the entire height, from the basement to the bell lantern, for the discharge of vitiated air from the building; a centre shaft, through which the bells were hoisted and in which the clock weights are suspended, which extends from the ground to the clock-room floor; the space on the east and north sides being occupied by record rooms, except the three lower stories which are on a level with those of the stories of the Sergeant-at-arms' residence, and are entered from them. These are the prison-rooms belonging to the House of Commons.'

Our guide stopped us at one of these doors, and announced that the last person to be held in this prison room was the suffragette Mrs Pankhurst, in 1902. A lively and learned-looking young woman spoke up : 'Excuse me, you must have got the date wrong. The Suffragette movement only became militant later; 1906 at the earliest.' '1902 I've been told, lady; I can't change it now'. 'I know it's wrong; I'm working on a study of the Movement, and besides, men always get their history wrong.'

The lady was right; there is no record of an occupant of the prison room since Charles Bradlaugh was detained there in 1880. Mrs Pankhurst naughtily threw a stone at a picture in St Stephen's Hall in 1913 and, according to her own account, was taken to 'a small police room in the inner precincts' until the House rose.

All the rest was sweetness, full of sound rather than light. We arrived in the machinery chamber for the

three-quarters chime. The whirring and the clatter made much more offensive a noise than that of the bells higher up, when we stood round them at midday. Thinking to be deafened for life, it was pleasant that the familiar noise left us all unscarred, even at close quarters.

Visits to the Clock Tower were discontinued after the murder of Airey Neave, just before the 1979 general election.

The heights of the three towers of the Palace of Westminster are : the Clock Tower 316 feet; the central tower above the octogon of the Central Lobby 300 feet; the Victoria Tower through whose archway the Sovereign arrives for the Opening of Parliament, 323 feet. All measured by Trinity House from low water mark in the tidal River Thames; a little unfair perhaps, in footage, to other erectile embellishments of the British Isles.

These are not the only Westminster Towers. Do not forget the Abbey, particularly Hawksmoor's West Towers, and the Parliamentary parish church of St. Margaret's, a much bigger church than its huge neighbours, the Abbey and Westminster Hall, would lead you to suppose.

The Palace of Westminster is nineteenth-century Gothic and was only fully opened in 1852. Sir Charles Barry and A. W. Pugin almost certainly got the inspiration for the Clock Tower from Pugin's delightful confection at Scarisbrick Hall, near Southport in Lancashire, which was, sadly, replaced by a monstrously tall horror by Pugin's son, the very much lesser E. W. Pugin.

Big Ben is the name only of the bell which strikes the hour, and is probably named after a fashionable pugilist, Benjamin Caunt.

The Wallace Monument, Stirling

This grotesque erection commands both respect and affection by its stony eminence and prominent siting. It rises 220 feet above the 300 foot Abbey Craig overlooking Stirling and its Castle. From the platform below the crown the view stretches from Ben Lawers to the Pentland Hills and exposes a great panorama of the Lowlands centred on the Forth Valley and its Firth, bounded to the north east by the Ochil Hills of Fife. Arthur's Seat above Edinburgh and the Forth Bridges are visible in clear weather. Stirling is not only 'the Gateway' between Highlands and Lowlands, it is the principal crossroads of Scotland.

The Wallace Monument was the invention of the Rev Dr Charles Rodgers, whose design was executed by the architect John T. Rochead of Glasgow. It looks almost as though the stone had arranged itself into this shape with its massive pinnacled crown, rather than that designers and craftsmen had been at work. It took from 1861–69 to build, from freestone quarried on the crag, and at one time lack of subscription money held up work.

Within a 36 ft square base, with immensely thick walls, there are four great vaulted chambers of equal dimensions one above another, in each of which are grouped different objects—armour, busts of other heroes, and the like. These halls are sombre, the light obscured by stained glass windows high in the walls.

The Monument makes a strong appeal to visitors, especially natives, for William Wallace was truly a national hero whose patriotism never deviated, never compromised. He harried Edward I's armies by guerrilla tactics until he was at last captured in 1305, brought to London and brutally executed at Smithfield after a brief trial.

The historian G. M. Trevelyan wrote of Wallace: 'This unknown knight, with little but his great name to identify him in history, had lit a fire which nothing since has ever put out . . . it had no name then, but now we should call it democratic patriotism . . . Theories of nationhood and theories of democracy would follow afterwards to justify or explain it. Meanwhile it stood up, a fact'.

Cardiff Castle: The Clock Tower

Cardiff Castle proper is the Norman Keep on its steep mound within the vast enclosure of the curtain walls, risen to their present scale and strength for little more than a hundred years, but following the lines of the Roman fortification of 1,700 years ago.

Along the west wall was a range of buildings where Capability Brown fiddled about with touches of eighteenth-century Gothick. Ninety years later two young men got busy.

The 3rd Marquess of Bute, who had succeeded to great estates at the age of six months, was still a minor when he asked William Burges, the architect son of one of the engineers who constructed Cardiff docks, to make a report on the reconstruction of the Castle. Lord Bute had all the money in the world; Burges and he were both filled with the expensive and florid anti-quarianism of that age. A partnership of two escapists from materialism.

The first consequence, and all that we are concerned with here, was the Clock Tower. It was designed as bachelor apartments for the young nobleman, one room above another. Work started in 1868, the year of his majority. Later it became the vertical male part of an extensive and richly decorated palace, every inch of floor and wall and ceiling tricked out in Gothical, mythical and pre-Raphaelitish fantasy.

Burges must have been in reaction from his father's engineering skill, though he too thoroughly understood the principles of construction; Lord Bute had sensations opposite to his predecessor's commercial acumen in developing Cardiff docks and city.

The result in the Clock Tower is the winter smoking room on the lowest level, with the signs of the Zodiac painted on the ceiling. Above that is the bachelors' bedroom. Here precious stones are painted on the frieze and named in art lettering so crafty as to be hard to decipher. The adjoining bath chamber squashes in a big rectangle of a Roman bath of marble. Inlaid on its sides are fishes. A newt crawls along the bottom.

On the third stage is a servant's room now got up as a Victorian kitchen. At the top is the summer smoking room with an open gallery above, within the four faces of the lantern. Here is a fine view of Cardiff Bay and the hills to the north. At every level there are heroic and symbolic murals whose execution, it must be admitted, is weak.

The smallness of the rooms is a surprise. Nobody could loll here in a leather chair with pipe or cigar and there is no room for that essential feature of a bachelor's wing—the billiards room. If you want the masculine sanctum of a Victorian house to stand so very erect you cannot have everything.

Bute and Burges also worked on Castell Coch in South Glamorgan, where the interiors are almost as rich and quaint as at Cardiff.

Westminster Cathedral Tower

The great campanile, St. Edward's Tower, of the mother church of England's Roman Catholics is a bold invitation to enter the Cathedral itself, so much more spacious and lofty than it appears from the outside. The total height of the Tower, 284 feet, exceeds Boston Stump by 12 feet. One up to the Romans. The Anglican Cathedral at Liverpool beats them both. The C. of E. wins the day.

At Westminster you are whisked up 185 feet, by a small lift, to the viewing platforms. These are four balconies, one on each face of the square Tower. A gentle aroma of incense wafts towards you and from some low modern buildings below steam evaporates from the heating and cooling plants. From the east balcony you get a clear idea of the Cathedral's plan with its four flattened domes, three for the nave and one for the Sanctuary, all in that pale viridescence of weathered copper.

The views are marred. The River Thames is hardly visible, the scene to east and south prickled by well-separated tower blocks. If only they were clustered, as the late great Professor A. E. Richardson said they should have been if they had to be there at all, the aesthetic effect would be less disastrous, but would the social consequences be even worse? To the west a huge monster across Victoria Street dominates all, to the north there is little sense of the deliberately contrasting style to the Gothic of the Abbey and the Houses of Parliament; they are mostly occluded by the glass and concrete of the new Victoria Street.

The architect, J. C. Bentley, had a sure genius for controlling masses on an awkward site, and in a style far removed from the Gothic Revival with which he had been hitherto associated. In 1894 Cardinal Manning insisted that the new cathedral should be in a style not Gothic, to avoid comparison with Westminster Abbey, and despite Bentley's refusal to enter his design in competition, both cardinal and architect were sure that they were right and Bentley was appointed.

Although he never joined the R.I.B.A. his design was awarded the Royal Gold Medal in 1902, but he died the day before the presentation ceremony. He could never have lived to see his work completed, for he was born in 1839 and it is barely completed yet. This strange compound of Byzantine, Romanesque Venetian and German influences is a lasting monument of originality, precision and adaptation to tiresome regulations.

The Post Office Tower, London

London's famous Post Office Tower does not quite reach the sky, but much of the bag of tricks within and on top of this glass-clad column is interested in that part of the sky called the ionosphere. The big idea is to convey all our chatter on the telephone by super-high-frequency radio links suitably bounced by the ionisphere to satellite towers and masts throughout the country. To the east and south-east to connect with Europe; to Birmingham—which has its own 350 foot concrete clad tower—and beyond; to Goonhilly and the Americas. Not much more than ten per cent of our calls are conveyed by means of this electronic engineering as yet; the rest of us put up with the present electro-mechanical system.

This is not all. The Tower also does technical monitoring of our TV systems and assists in network switching, helps the Met. Service with its radar storm-warning scanner, a sort of revolving saucer just below the topmost mast. The Post Office is also developing its own system of putting information, at the fingering of a dial, on a TV screen. Their engineers and their computer promise a much greater supply of useless information than that offered at present by the systems of the BBC and IBA.

Now, a few figures and more facts. From pavement to pop-up aerial the height is 620 feet. The restaurant, which revolves during mealtimes, is only 520 feet up. There are 13,000 tons of concrete, steel and glass combined, nothing compared to the weight of Borthwick Castle. The foundations go down twenty-four feet. A three-foot-thick concrete raft floats on a layer of oil spread on the blue London clay. On the raft is a flattened pyramid of concrete of which the top sticks up one foot above ground. Then all that glass and steel and concrete.

The real magic is in the complex structure above. All successful towers should sway in the breeze. This is undesirable for the P.O. Tower, because the aerials must stay accurate to within one third of a degree. The equipment inside does not mind deviation, but the aerials, and the attendant engineers, do. So ingenuity of architect and engineer combined to design a tower of more than ordinary rigidity. So it is, and let nobody accuse the Post Office Corporation of a kind of priapism, so long as the telephone service, by 1995 it is estimated, is fully electronic.

There is no public access except to the restaurant, which is expensive.

Liverpool: Two Cathedrals

To Liverpool, then, on a sunny Sunday, by train. The principal object in view the Anglican Cathedral Church of Christ. On the way there were many advance notices—small exclamation marks in the landscape—of churches built in red sandstone, but nothing to warn of the scale of one of the largest, as well as one of the newest, cathedrals in the world.

Competition for the design was won by Giles Gilbert Scott, grandson of the busy Victorian restorer, at the age of 22. In 1904 Edward VII laid the foundation stone; in October 1978 Elizabeth II was present at a service to celebrate its completion. A short time compared with most cathedrals, but in an age of hurry and doubt many questioned whether the expensive and expansive work should continue.

Even during the two world wars building did not altogether stop. During World War II, Giles Scott set the last stone on the topmost pinnacle of the tower, 347 feet up. The construction of this vast thing had been made possible by a large donation from the Vestey family and it is known as the Vestey Tower. There seems to be a kinship between the good red meat on which the Vestey fortune is based and the colour of the entire edifice.

On a high commanding site, backed by Liverpool's best Georgian terraces, the elephantine mass of red masonry is held together by the Vestey Tower. Architectural scholars must one day give me their opinion of the strangely diminished pinnacles, no more prominent than the ear tufts of an owl in relation to the whole.

Were the owls wise to go on, stage by stage, as money was subscribed, to carry Sir Giles Scott's often changing plans to completion? Could the enormous amount needed have been better spent for the benefit of secular Liverpool? Well, yes; but in that case it probably would not have been offered.

Along a straight street to the north, which still shows evidence of classical Liverpool, is the Roman Catholic Cathedral of Christ the King. Work began in 1933 on the plan of Edwin Lutyens for an even larger Byzantine church than the Anglican Gothic. No more than the crypt is now there. There was a long hiatus, and then Cardinal Heenan, at that time Archbishop of Liverpool, got things moving. Frederick Gibberd's plan was accepted in 1959. It must be built within 10 years, with room for 3000. It was done by 1967, for not much more than a million pounds.

The circular big top, mosaic clad to give better weathering than its concrete frame, elevates to a spike-topped lantern, which is nearly all glass. It is sometimes known as Paddy's lantern. The abstractions of John Piper's windows reflect light in psychedelic colours throughout the body of the church. Other windows do the same, flecks and splashes of a chemical rainbow. It is all a bit disturbing. The graceful crucifix on the central

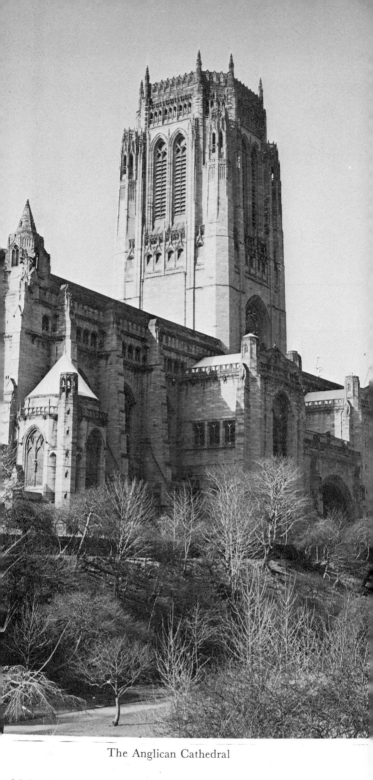

The Anglican Cathedral

high altar is a thin masterpiece by Elizabeth Frink.

On that sunny Sunday Evensong was just beginning at the Anglican Cathedral, so we tactfully withdrew to the Roman Cathedral where Benediction was just ending. In either church there was good singing by the choir, and a small congregation.

The street linking the two is called Hope, always has been. Sir Giles Scott was a Catholic, Sir Frederick Gibberd is not. Those presiding over the two Cathedrals are friendly. If hope leads to unity, and we are all joined in the Universal Church, which will become redundant?

ACKNOWLEDGEMENTS

For help of many kinds my thanks are due to people too numerous to list in full, particularly those to whom a tower belongs or who, in a sense, belong to a tower. For hospitality and advice in the course of long and often dreary journeys on motorways and the more agreeable sort of road I am grateful to Margaret Aberdeen, Keith Gatley, Mr. and Mrs. Bill Hugonin, Alvilde and James Lees-Milne, Sarah and Patrick Scott, Diana and Antony Sperling and Norman Whitfield. In addition to hospitality, chauffeuring was a comfort from Joanna Gordon, June Gordon, Esther Grainger, Alfhild Hansen, Jessamine and Michael Harmsworth and Charles Pagen. Welcome and necessary advice, the gift and loan of books and other source material were provided by Anthony Barker, John Betjeman, Antony Derville, Lord Gladwyn, Desmond Guinness, Janet Hitchman, the late John Lloyd, Norman Scarfe and Robert Wolrige-Gordon. The editorial hand of Roy Gasson has been necessarily firm but never unfriendly, and the typing of Mrs. Mair a great improvement on my two-finger exercises. Finally I am grateful to Frame Hastings for her perpetual encouragement and enthusiasm. In a way, she started it all.

PICTURE CREDITS

Picture research : Enid Moore

Aerofilms Ltd., 103; John Bangay, 52–3; Barnaby's Picture Library, 13, 27(C), 35(T), 43, 45(T), 111; John Bethell, 25(C), 39(B); J. Bryant & Sons, 97(T); Courtauld Institute of Art, 57; by courtesy of Mr. Alan Howe, City of Edinburgh District Council, 71(B); A. F. Kersting, Frontispiece, 18, 21, 23, 29, 37, 49, 51, 55(T), 63(T), 67, 77(R), 83(T), 85, 93, 97(B), 107; The Mansell Collection, 35(B), 99, 101; National Monuments Record, 15, 17, 31, 45(B), 47, 59, 61(T), 77(L), 91(B); The National Trust, 25(B); The National Trust for Scotland, 73, 81, 87; by courtesy of the Post Office, 109; The Powell-Cotton Museum, 89(TR); Radio Times Hulton Picture Library, 10, 25(T), 27(T), 63(B), 65, 89(B); by courtesy of St. Bride's church, 75; Mervyn Rees, 95; Royal Commission on the Ancient and Historical Monuments of Scotland, 69; Royal Commission on Ancient and Historical Monuments in Wales, 27(B); The Librarian, Royal Institute of British Architects, 83(B), 91(TR), 105(B); The Scotsman Publications Ltd., 71(T); Scottish Development Department, Edinburgh (Crown Copyright Reserved), 39(T); Thomas Photos, 55(B).